D1860300

BETWEEN THE TWILIGHTS

BETWEEN THE TWILIGHTS

BEING STUDIES OF INDIAN WOMEN BY ONE OF THEMSELVES

CORNELIA SORABJI

GYAN

Published by

Gyan Publishing House
5, Ansari Road
Daryaganj, New Delhi-110002
Phone: 011-47034999, 9811692060
E-mail: books@gyanbooks.com

Distribution Network
gyanbooks.com
India, USA, Canada, UK, Australia, France

© Publisher

All rights reserved. No part of this work may be reproduced, stored, adapted, or transmitted in any form or by any means, electronic, mechanical, photocopying, micro-filming, recording or otherwise, or translated in any language, without the prior written permission of the copyright owner and the publisher.

ISBN : 978-81-212-9090-6 (PB)
First Published, 1908

2nd Impression 2023

Printed at: Gyan Press, Delhi.

The book is sold subject to the condition that it shall not, by way of trade or otherwise, be lent, resold, hired out, or otherwise circulated without the prior publisher's written consent.

BETWEEN THE TWILIGHTS

AUTHOR: CORNELIA SORABJI

BETWEEN THE TWILIGHTS: BEING STUDIES OF INDIAN WOMEN BY ONE OF THEMSELVES

BY

CORNELIA SORABJI

1908

DEDICATED

TO

THE HOUR OF UNION

PREFACE

IN the language of the Zenana there are two twilights, "when the Sun drops into the sea," and "when he splashes up stars for spray," . . . the *Union*, that is, *of Earth and Sun, and*, again, *of Light and Darkness.*

And the space between is the time of times in these sun-wearied plains in which I dwell. One sees the world in a gentle haze of reminiscence—reminiscence of the best. There, across the horizon, flames the Sun's "good-bye." Great cave of mystery, or lake of liquid fire: anon pool of opal and amethyst, thoughts curiously adjustable to the day that is done, memory of joy or sorrow, of strength of love, or disregard of pain. Gradually the colour fades, now to a golden fleece of the softest, now to wisps of translucence, blush-pink, violet: oft-times the true ecstasy of colour is in the east, away from the Sun's setting. Or, now again, the sky is a study in grays and blue-grays, in that peculiar heat-haze which belongs to May and September, and the pale curve of the new moon looks old and weary. Is not all Life marching towards the Silence? it seems to say.

Yes, the manner of its loitering is varied, but always, always, is it an hour of enchantment, this hour Between the Twilights: and it is my very own. I choose it, from out the day's full sheaf, and I sit with it in the Silences on my roof-tree.

It was in this hour, through a hot summer, that the thoughts which make this little book came to me, and were written down. I had spent my days going in and out among my friends of the Zenana, and a great yearning was in my heart that others should know them as I did, in their simplicity and their wisdom.

The half is not yet told: much would not bear telling—I had no business to take strangers into the walled garden of our intimacy—and some things were too elusive for speech, but the sounds which have thridded the Silence have been echoes of reality, and I can only hope that they may convey some impression of the gently pulsing life of the Zenana.

Not by any means are the Studies meant to be exhaustive. I have left out of count the Anglicized and English-educated Indian, the capable woman who earns her own living, the cultured woman of the world or philanthropist. There was little to learn about her which a common language and the opportunity of intercourse might not teach any sojourner in India at first-hand.

But these others of whom I have written seemed to justify in a very special sense the hour of my meditation. . . . They float elusive in the half-light between two civilizations, sad by reason of something lost, sad by reason of the more that may come to be rejected hereafter. . . . And none but God knoweth when will toll for them that final Hour of Union, and whether, when it is here, we shall be able to see the stars through the blue veil of the Light that lies slain for all Eternity.

CONTENTS

* "Portraits of some Indian Women" is reprinted from "The Nineteenth Century and After," by the kind permission of the late Sir J. Knowles.

GLOSSARY

Amla, officer of a household.

Bina, a musical instrument (stringed).

Brahmin, highest or priestly caste.

Didi, elder sister.

Guru, spiritual guide.

Jog, Hindu Vedantic system of meditation and of acquiring sanctity.

Kincab, gold brocade.

Khattriya, the fighter: of the fighting or second highest Caste.

Mali, gardener.

Mantras, incantations.

Munias, small speckled birds.

Namascar, the salutation to the learned: and to a superior.

Pandas, pilgrim guides at holy places.

Pooja, worship of a God.

Pujari, a Temple servant.

Purdahnashin, she who sits behind the curtain: the secluded.

Sais, groom.

Saree, a long winding-sheet, which forms the drapery worn by women.

Shastras, sacred writings.

Sudra, the server; of the fourth or Serving Class.

Takht-posh, a wooden plank on four legs used as a bedstead.

Veishya, originally of the third or agricultural, now often of the professional caste.

BETWEEN THE TWILIGHTS

I

THE STORY OF WISDOM

SHE comes with the Spring—a two days' guest in an Indian household. Nor has frequency bred either carelessness or coolness of reception. Early on the morning of her arrival you will see the women hastening from the Bathing Ghat, their garments clinging about their supple limbs, their long hair drying in the wind. They bear full water-pots, for nought but Gunga-Mai to-day suffices—no slothful backsliding to near-by pump.

In the house of my friend, it was Parvati, the oldest serving-woman who undertook to make ready the guest chamber. I watched her as she crossed the courtyard—a handful of the precious liquid for Dharti-Mai the Earth Mother, and the rest—a generous swob, for the black marble veranda. Soon had she helpers, and to spare—the most practised among them made the white chalk marks of good luck—tridents, fishes, flames of fire; and the tidiest made the little inclosure—white cotton "railings," the posts being balls of Ganges mud, in which were buried swiftly-flying arrows—threat for daring devil.

But the centre of interest was naturally the Altar. This was just a plain raised platform of wood, carrying bravely its variety of offering. Great mountains of yellow and white flowers, with fruits, chiefly the cocoanut, fruit of healing, old Sanskrit manuscripts, lettered palm-leaves, thumbed and blotted copybooks and tattered "primers"—the prayers of children—the pointed reed, and ink-horns, glass ink-pots and steel pens from the "Europe" shop across the way; a school edition of "The Vicar of Wakefield," Ganot's Physics, quaint combs and mirrors, powder-boxes, and perfumes, "the tears of scented grass," or that more subtle "scent of red rose leaves." Why not? Is she not woman, even though a Goddess and learned? The "Europe" products, I notice, carry milk in place of ink. "Sanctify to us this Western Education"—is that what it means in this country, where deepest feeling finds outlet other than through doors of speech? So her worshippers made ready, not in private chapel but here where the life of the days pulsed and languished through the years; here, where friend or passing stranger might alike turn to greet her; for Wisdom is one, though her hosts be many. Moreover, She who is called Wisdom loves the voices of little children, and nothing is hushed, or ordered otherwise for her coming. The most unregenerate rogue romps at her feet, the most thriftless housewife, the most rebellious daughter-in-law has access to her Altar, and through the day one after another will come bearing her gift; and, lingering a while, will go away softly even as she came. Sometimes, by no means generally, there will be an image of the Goddess. One such I have seen in the house of a rich merchant. It was a life-sized figure dancing on a lotus, the full bloom, pink-edged, in her hand she bore a *bina*, for the Goddess of Wisdom is also Queen of Harmony; and the rich man's friends had honoured her as was meet, with priceless gifts of *Kincab*, of gem, of trinket. Now Wisdom of necessity has yet one more aspect, she is Goddess of

Perfect Speech. It is of her that the tongue-tied prays eloquence, the scholar success; and the offering to her in this capacity you will find absent from no Altar, rich or poor. To omit this would mean the curse of the dumb for ever. It is a little cake of rice and milk, this oblation for lapses from accuracy, for "benevolent falsehood."

"Oh Guest of the hours, remember the past, the puzzling need of the tangled moments, remember—and forgive."

A list of benevolent falsehoods must needs vary with the age. Manu includes (viii, 130) "The giver of false evidence for a pious motive, for such an one shall not lose a seat in heaven," his lapses being called the "Speech of the Gods."

"To save a life," "To protect a cow," "To counteract the thriftless ways of husbands," have added Hindu women of my acquaintance.

Simple is the ritual of the worship of Wisdom. "With folded hands I bow before the Goddess, the Goddess who provides all wealth, and vouchsafes the power of speech." "May the Goddess of Wisdom protect me, the Mother of the Vedas, who from the crimson lotus of her hands pours radiance on the implements of writing, and on the works produced by her power."

"May the Goddess of Wisdom protect me— She who robed in white, sets far all ignorance. She who abides with the Creator may she abide with me . . .;" and the rest of the prayers are either said by the Priest, or found in the heart of the worshipper. The battered lesson book, the oft-used pen, are these not prayers in themselves?

The last time I saw the Goddess was at the Children's Festival. Wisdom danced on her lotus flower, in a little bower of bamboos and marigolds, out in the open courtyard. At her feet sat children, row upon row, ranging in age from three years to twelve. I watched them come so happily, tripping hand in hand with some friend or comrade. They wore their best gay little saree, gold-spangled and bordered, in their hair thread of gold, or great heavy ornament, or just some flower among the light close braidings. And, as they took their seats in the Great Cathedral roofed by God's sky, the Priests moved among them anointing each little forehead with oil of sandal wood from off the altar of her who is named Wisdom.

Then the musicians beat their drums and rang the bell of worship, and every single forehead was on the ground before the Goddess. The worship had begun. . . . First be consecrate, then bring your offering—is the creed. . . . I heard no prayers, but thereafter, one by one, the Babies passed before her, throwing at her feet sweet-scented wreaths of Jasmine. I needed not then to hear their prayers. . . . And that was all the Service. The play of the children at the feet of Wisdom.

Thus then the Hindu honours his Guest. And, on the second day—for even Wisdom must share at length the waters of oblivion —with music and singing with the happy laughter of children and a gay following of the faithful, her image is taken to the Ganges; and with love and much injunction as to next year's journey from the Mounts of Blessing, is it set afloat on that sacred river whose bourne is the Eternal Sea.

Wisdom, in Sanskrit story, is Creative

Power to the Great God himself, his energy —without her he is but a great incommunicable passive force.

"I make strong whom I choose—originating all things I pass even as a breeze. Above the Heavens am I, beyond the Earth, and what is the Great One, *that* am I. I make holy the Great God Himself. For the Great Archer it is I bend the bow; it is I who stay evil in the name of the Destroyer. Few know me, yet near to all alike am I. God is he from whom Wisdom and Speech—after reaching Him—return."

Unravelling it all, what quaint teaching may we not piece together? That is true wisdom which puts man in touch with God—creature with Creator. And the same power of God refrains not from blessing the things that are of value to the Earth—the written, the spoken word, all arts and harmonies and science.

Then, is it not a parable that the Goddess of Speech is primarily the Goddess of all Learning? Let the ignorant keep silence.

The *Tulsi* spirals stirred in the hot wind, and the great white red-throated Sarus flapped his wings as he walked about the women's courtyard. The men of the house had taken the Image to the water, and we sat by the empty altar in the hour between the Twilights. "Tell me more about Wisdom," said I to my Wisest of the Wise, and she told me of how Vishnu gave her as wife to Brahma, and how Brahma put a slight upon the Lady of Wisdom—a slight which she never forgave.

A great sacrifice was going forward, and the Priest bade Brahma call his Lady. For is it not the wife, and she alone who must hold the sacred grass, must sprinkle the offerings. "But Saraswati is engaged in dressing," was the answer.

Then the Priest "without a wife what blessing can come?"

So Brahma turned to Indra, and bade him find a substitute in hedge or highway.

Indra soon returned, leading by the hand a milkmaid, beautiful and happy. She bore a jar of butter on her head. "She shall become the Mother of the Vedas," said the Priest; and that is how Gayatri, the Milkmaid, was wed to the Great God Himself.

Then came forth Saraswati all unconscious,

and very gorgeous, attended by the wives of Vishnu, Rudra, and other of the Gods—a worthy train.

When she heard what had happened, she was wroth beyond power of words to tell.

Said the Great God, shamefaced, "The Priest did this thing; the Priest and Indra."

But Saraswati said, "By the powers I have obtained, may Brahma never be worshipped in Temple or Sacred Place—except one day in each year—and since Indra, thou didst bring that Milkmaid to my Lord, thou shalt be bound in chains by all thine enemies and prisoned in a strange and distant country, thy power over the winds and thy station on high, given to others. Cursed also be ye—Priests. Henceforth shall ye perform sacrifices solely for the desire of obtaining the usual gifts, and for love of gain alone shall ye serve Temples and holy places; satisfied only shall ye be with the food of others, and dissatisfied with that of your own houses. And in quest of riches shall ye unduly perform rites and ceremonies." . . .

In great wrath she called for her peacock, to leave the assembly, but the Goddess of Wealth refused to accompany her; and her also did she curse.

"May you always abide with the vile and the inconstant, the contemptible and foolish, the sinful, cruel and vulgar."

After her departure Gayatri modifies all the curses; so neither need all Priests nor all the wealthy be base and contemptible.

When the youngest daughter-in-law in the house is listening to the story-telling my Wisest of the Wise adds a variation—Saraswati is appeased, and Brahma says he will do with the Milkmaid what the Goddess commands, while the Milkmaid herself falls at the feet of Wisdom, who, raising her, says, "Let be—let you and me both serve my Lord!"

* * * * *

And now for a year her Altar is empty but she is not forgotten, and in the practice and devotion of the faithful still does the third watch of the night belong to Wisdom.

"Let the home-keeping ones wake in the time sacred to Saraswati, the Goddess of Speech; let them reflect on virtue and virtuous emoluments; and on the whole meaning and essence of the words of Wisdom."

* * * * *

"So desirable, and yet she may be only a two days' Guest in a Hindu household," I mused aloud.

"Ah, but," answered she who worshipped Wisdom, "were Wisdom always with us, how should we live among the sons of men!" . . .

II

THE STORY OF DESTRUCTION

WHEN the world was young there were two Giant Demons—Shumbo and Nishumbo, who made great discord both in heaven and upon earth: nor did victory bring harmony, for when all who opposed them lay vanquished, they fought with each other.

Then did the Gods and Godlings take counsel how they might slay them. "Go to the Destroyer," said the Great God, and so said also the Preserver—"It is his business." But Shiva, the Destroyer, owned to a dilemma. "I have promised them," said he, "that no *man* shall prevail against them. What shall I do?" Then upon meditation—"I am resolved what to do. One shall I create in the form of a woman, that this strife might be ended." . . .

And that was how Creation came near to

Kali the Mother. Very beautiful was she, the strength of the strong, and the attractiveness of that which was to conquer strife: and her did Shiva name *Jugatdatri*—Nurse of the World. None could stand before her, and it came to pass that at last was left only one enemy—the King of Demons; and he, seeing her beauty, sought her in marriage; but she laughed saying, "I wed none but him I cannot conquer."

And Shumbo maddened by her laughter vowed victory, and her very glory was a peril, for he seized upon her hair, and impeded her much. . . . Then did the Gods take counsel again together. It was the Destroyer who found help.. "Let us each give her of our strength," said he, "that evil may be smitten for ever."

And they did all even as he suggested, and the incoming of this great strength made her so that she lost some of her comeliness. And now was she called *Kali* . . . She that is black.

And the strength of the Gods was as wine to her, and she fought intoxicate. And behold, while all the Gods and Demons watched, they fought—those two—the Nurse of the World and the King of Evil, and Kali won.

Then was there great rejoicing on earth and in heaven, and Kali joyed no less than her creatures, and she danced in her joy, drunk with the blood of her victim.

And for the third time the Gods took counsel, for they said, "The thing we have ourselves made strong will at last destroy even us."

And the Great God said: "She is wife to the Destroyer. This is his business." And Shiva thought long and earnestly, for even he could not causelessly retake the strength that he had given. . . . And the end of the meditation was that he went forth from Heaven and lay in her path as she came down from the Snow mountains in her dance of Death. And she, mad with victory and blood, seeing nothing, danced on to his chest exultant, when looking down, she recognized her husband, and was shamed and sobered. And this final vision of Kali is the one worshipped by her children —Kali, the four-armed, the Conqueror of Demons, vanquished only by the husband who lies under her feet. In one hand beareth she the head of a victim, in another a sword, with a third she blesseth, and with the fourth she holdeth out fearlessness to all her followers. She wears a garland of skulls, and a waistlet of hands,—and no more danceth she the dance of Death. Yet to her, the Mother, come alike all who are drunk with blood, righteous or unrighteous, for she understands; and all who would have the strength of the Gods to slay the Evil in the world—for was not this the purpose of her being, in the old, old days when the world was young? . . .

Thus to me one of my gentle friends of "The Inside" in this land of legend and silences.

Then we turned to her of many years and long meditations, who sat by listening—"Is that how you know the story, Mother?"

"Yea, my children," made she answer. "Even so—and when mine eyes are shut these are the thoughts that come to me—blessing and cursing, destruction and creation, death and life—are not both companions of Time?"

"But the skull and hands, Mother—read that parable."

And she—"All is destroyed save intelligence and work—these outlast us."

So, museful, I took my way to the Mount of Kali, which lies without the City, past many ancient tanks grown rank with vegetation, past flowering trees, and swamps of mat huts and malaria.

A bright-eyed baby played upon a log, see-sawing over a nauseous drain—Was this one measure of the dance of Death? . . . An avenue now of shops—the Precincts—Gods and Godlings and sacrificial vessels were for sale, with the beads of the Sacred, and water-bottles made of Ganges sand blown fine as glass. . . . I lingered among the women making purchase. Images of Kali seemed most popular, with bright red and yellow horses for the children, nor was the picture shop neglected—and I laughed softly to myself to see a German print of Romeo and Juliet in the balcony scene selling clamorously for "Radha Krishna," the gay God with his favourite lady.

Seated under a *pipal* tree, hoary with age, was an ash-smeared Priest, at his feet a heap of yellow marigolds. No woman passed him without some offering, and sometimes he spoke, but most often kept silence, noting all things through the matted hair that veiled his slits of eyes. Of such begging Priests there was a great collection—the ascetics sat still, but were gifted for fear of curses; others ran after the women, teasing, traducing each other; and these were gifted for their importunity. One, half-mad, I think, had a few words of English and followed me cursing the Priest-guide I had chosen for a "stupid-'umbug-flatterer"—said all as one long word, which sounded a potent curse indeed.

The Image is in a small brick and stone building behind closed doors, which are opened at fixed times. In the ante-room sit the faithful, reading sacred books or preparing their offerings for the Goddess. There seemed a separate Priest for each devotee.

One man only did I see whom my heart convicted of holiness: and looking on his face I knew that it was possible even here to forget all the grossness to which the ignorant had degraded the Kali-legend. . . . The place of Sacrifice ran red, and already the Priests had sold the flesh of Kali's tale of goats to eager bidders. The poorer applicants sat in a circle, a gory head on each lap. . . . It was a gruesome sight.

By the Bathing Ghat was a great crowd. Here were two young women in charge of a chaperone. They had come far ways measuring their length along the ground. It was in the rains, and they were all mud and slush from the exercise. The woman stood by, policing them, seeing that they abated no jot or tittle of their vows, where the head had been the feet should lie—there, and not an inch further.

"What was the vow?" I asked.

A prayer for one—that the child then on its way might live. . . . Oh! the pathos of it. The other woman was giving thanks for the recovery of her reason. . . . "The dance of Death," "The dance of Death"—a minuet. . . .

"If I were God, I should pity the heart of man . . ."

They were travelling at the moment towards the drain behind the Image of the Goddess. Oh! the water, oh! the water!—it was black with impurities. It had washed the feet of the

Goddess, and the flowers of her Temple, and the refuse of the Sacrifice; but they drank eagerly—at full length still—content.

It was a parable on the power of Faith. . . . And truly, the Temple of Kali opens many doors to reflection. Evil, we notice, is conquered by Time in the end. Of Love, which conquered Time, there is no Gospel in Hinduism. Inherent strength is the last vanquisher, the Great Gods themselves helping in the conquest, even parting with their own strength to the fighter. And that which God inspires may be as God. Yet, in spite of the Hindu doctrine of works, there would seem to be a caution against too great activity. Kali drunk with activity was shamed by Gods and men. . . .

* * * * *

I went back to my Wise Woman of many years. . . . "To the ignorant," she said, "Kali but wants a life—Kali slays and Kali makes alive. Said I not once before, blessing and cursing, death and life, these are the Soul's eternal doors. In the house of Kali the doors are ever open. . . . But, for us women, the lesson to hide in the heart is this —Kali, the Great Destroyer, the Nurse of the

World, the Dread-Inspirer, is vanquished only by—her husband."

* * * * *

Here, then, meet ancient story and modern history, the history of every Hindu woman throughout the Land. The last stage of perfection is wifely submission.

III

THE STORY OF A WOMAN

NOW Dokhio, the Father of Durga, was wroth because Shiva, to whom he had given his daughter in marriage, though he had the reputation of a God, was as poor as any beggar. And in his wrath he devised revenge. He made a great Feast, to which he bade Gods and Goddesses, Godlings and baby Godlings—all, save Shiva and his wife Durga. And Narod, the Mischief Man, was made the voice to bear the message to each guest.

So Narod went to Shiva, and "This is what your Father-in-law hath planned," saith he, inciting.

But Shiva, "What is that to me?" "Dishonour, insult, affront—see you not?" said the Mischief Man.

And Shiva, again, "What is that to me? They who do not honour cannot hurt me." . .

Narod then went to Durga, Shiva's wife: "A Feast of Gods and Goddesses," saith he. "Let be," said Durga; "What is that to me?"

"Such display of dresses and jewels, such cackling of women's tongues. 'Why is Shiva not there? Why not Durga?' Surely a daughter may go to the house of her Father, by chance, on the day of the Feast, ignorant of what is forward?" . . .

Durga sought her husband. But he was firm. "They will make sport of you to spite me."

"What matter? It were worse not to be seen there—things happening behind our backs." . . .

But Shiva was firm.

Then did Durga use all the wiles of women —coaxing, sulking, flattering—Shiva was firm; so, finally she used the wiles of a more than human . . .

She took unto herself ten forms each more awful than the last, and ten-headed she passed before Shiva, threatening and mocking. Till —"Go!" said Shiva; "Let happen what will happen."

And Durga, a little fearfully, in that she

had got at last her heart's desire, arrayed herself in garments gorgeous and becoming, and made her way to her Mother's house. And her Mother embraced her right gladly, so that a great contempt was in Durga's heart for the trouble at which she had been in coming.

But the Mother said within herself: "It is well my Lord is away and busy, it is well . . . else might he hurt this child of mine."

Yet soon the question came: "And where is my Father?"

"At the Place of Sacrifice, where he makes a great feast," said the gentle Mother. "Stay with me, my child; leave such-like things to the men-people."

But Durga: "A Feast? Nay, then must I go and see" . . . and she heeded nothing.

And Dokhio was furious, in that after all his insult would be robbed of point.

"Why art thou come hither?" he thundered. And she: "Because my Father's daughters may not be kept from my Father's Sacrifice."

Then Dokhio cursed Shiva and all that belonged to him, which Durga hearing, passed out of life with grief inconsolable.

And Shiva, who had cared nothing for the slight to himself, revenged the death of his wife most mightily. He sent forth his lightning and consumed that great sacrifice ere they who were bidden had arrived to make it; and so the guests found nothing save charred wood, and a wizened old Dokhio with the head of a bearded goat.

For this was Shiva's little joke to keep the matter for ever in the mind of Durga's Father, Dokhio.

* * * * *

We sat on the great quiet roof in the cow-dust hour while the latest Mother-in-law among us told the story.

She meant it, I think, for the special benefit of Boho, the ten-year-old Bride; and she was gratified, for Boho caught her breath in great gusts at this bold coercion of a husband. Nothing did the story mean to her save that—punishment for such sacrilege.

But Kamalamoni looked up smiling from a game with the household tyrant—her Nagendra—aged four.

"It is not thus the story hath its ending," she said.

"Then tell the rest, Kamal." But Kamal was better occupied.

"And how calls the horse, my son? and how the dog? and the cat? and sheep? And," roguishly—"and how the great grandmother when in anger?" Till she of many years claimed Nagendra as her fee for such impertinence and Kamala was forced to tell her tale.

"And how should story end which wails no dirge for death of wife?" said Kamala, hotly. For opinion is but experience crystallized. "When Durga's soul left her body thus early, it wandered to the mountains of snow, and finding on the threshold of sense, the empty house of a new-born babe, it entered it."

Uma was the name by which its parents chose to know the child; and Uma grew strong and beautiful, gentle and good, with no memory of Durga the Ten-Headed. . . . And, one day when she had come to her woman's estate in our kingdom of life, and was playing with her waiting-woman among the swans beside the lotus-beds, an aged Priest-man appeared before her, and falling at her feet, said, "Durga Mother, thy Lord of

Destruction fasts and prays sorrowing for thee: go and tend him."

And Uma ran to her mother, wrathful. . . . "An old Priest-man fell at my feet Mother," she said, "and said unto me words which are not fit to be heard by me before my maidens."

So Uma's Father went out forthwith, and finding Narod—for he it was, the Mischief Man turned Priest in old-age, he heard the wondrous God-news about his daughter.

Shiva, it seemed lived a life of prayer and fasting—close by in the Cave of the Cow's mouth.

"Send Uma to tend him," said Narod, "and haply he will look and love, and they be man and wife once more."

Thus Uma was sent to Shiva, and tended him night and day; and the woman's love for the thing that she tended, grew in her heart.

But Shiva, full of self-pity for loss of a jewel which he might better have preserved (for this was his thought), saw not that same jewel lying burnished and re-beautified in the dust at his feet. And Uma's heart was sad, till even the Great God himself was moved to pity, and sent the little God of Love to wake

Shiva the Monk from his trance of bead-telling.

Then, fearfully—for is not Shiva the Destroyer himself?—went the Godling of the arched bow, and hiding in the bracken he shot forth his arrows—not without success. And Shiva, furious, saw one upturned foot in flight, and the fire from his eye burnt up the thing he saw, so that Kama Deva comes no more among the haunts of men.

But, and when his anger was dead, he looked up, and his eyes being opened, he beheld Uma, knowing her for Durga his own possession.

And so, once more was fulfilled the destiny of a woman.

"But for three days in every year does Uma go back to her parents and her swanlets in the mountains of Snow; and this journeying of Uma is always at *Durga-pooja* time when we make feast for many days to worship the Ten-handed."

In the silence which fell upon us after this story, she of many years was heard to yawn, while all the women snapped their fingers till her jaws met again.

From Shiva's Temple gleaming white among the yellow-green of the date palms came the sound of the *pooja* bell—some one, a woman probably, praying for her Lord to the Lord of Killing and Cursing. Clear against the gray-blue sky stood the cross-crowned spire of the Christian Cathedral; and almost at our doors, rang out the prayer-keeper's call to the faithful Moslem: "There is no God so great as God." . . .

"There is no God so great as—my God." It is what we are all saying; and it makes at once the strength and the tragedy of human lives. "No God so great as my God." What different things we mean when we say that—we of the bustling outside world.

The Hindu woman means one thing only. . . . "No God so great as my God." That was the lesson each was taking from the story of Durga and Uma. Did not almost every fable and legend chant that chorus? "No God so Great." . . . In punishment may be sometimes, or in penitence (see the miracle of the Destroyer himself turned monk for Durga) —but most of all in *graciousness*. . . .

"He knew Uma for her who went to

Dokhio's feast, and yet he forgave," said Boho Rani, "Oh! the wonder." . . .

But the Mother of Nagendra laughed, sure of her possession. . . . "The Godling of the arrows was not really burnt," she said, "the flying foot belonged to Kama's sheaf-bearer and rival, the less-than-godlet of unlawful love." . . .

And the Wise Woman smiled to herself in the growing dusk. "The ignorant are incapable of receiving knowledge," was what she said.

IV

DEVI—GODDESS!

A YOUNG unmarried girl is by some in Bengal called *Kumari*—Princess, and when married, *Devi*—Goddess.

I was musing on this, and all it told of the feeling of a Nation, and of the true beauty of that feeling at its best, when an old Prime-Minister friend of mine in a Native State came to invite me to a Ceremony.

It is known how I love all things primitive and individual, and my orthodox Hindu friends are very good to me in remembering this. "But of course I will come," I promised. "What is it this time?"

"The worship of young girls," said he. There was the idea again, the central idea in all Hindu thought in relation to women. . . . The worship of the *Life-Bringer*.

It was very simple, as all such Ceremonies

are, and free from all manner of false shame or conventionality. There was remembrance of the Creator; for the creature—the gentle little girls, such babies all of them—there were garlands of gay flowers, feastings and anointings with perfume of rose-leaves.

There was also towards them in the manner of these kindly elders who had long looked on the face of Nature, a pretty dignity and reverence which could not fail to beautify the fact of Creation whenever it should draw nigh.

Not long after, the youngest Bride in the household—she is but ten years of age—had a joy-making on her own account. She worshipped the Aged. They came in happy groups, the same who had so lately blessed her—toothless grandmother, great-aunt, cousins' Mother, wife of Mother-in-Law's Spiritual Guide—each had a name of her own in the dictionary of relationships. She received them charmingly, standing at the head of the Zenana stairs—the baby-hostess! falling at the feet (*parnam*) of those to whom she owed this courtesy, saluting others with joined hands raised to forehead (*numuscar*), and each made answer "Blessings," hand on the child's head. Then they sat in rows on little mats along the floor, and ate sweets and vegetables off green plantain leaves, their hostess waiting on them.

This little exchange of religious obligation is all the etiquette, and makes all the social amenities known among orthodox women in India.

It is hard to convey the idea, state the fact as one may, but the Hindu woman acknowledges no claims save those of religion. No social, no communal claims. Her worship of the Gods, of her husband, her children, they are all the same, part of her religion, and they make her life.

Even the ordinary business of the day, bathing, dressing, eating, is a religious act. . . . To cook her husband's food an orthodox Hindu wears a special silk garment: the only gardening she ever attempts is to water and tend the sacred basil (*Tulsi*). If she travels, it is on a pilgrimage to this shrine or that, to bathe in this or that sacred river. Of course she gives dinner parties as did my ten-year-old Bride, on special occasions, or on feasts of Gods and Goddesses through the year, also in memory of the dead; but there is no machinery of calls, no social entertaining for entertainment sake, no interchange of civilities to acquaint young people and make marriages. Marriages are made by the Priests and your map of stars, not by the social broker. For births and deaths you may have a house full of women, your relations or "spiritual" relations, come unbidden on a visit of congratulation or sympathy. To these you may never suggest departure, and only innate good manners in the visitor has saved from bankruptcy many a house in which the doors of Life and Death were often open.

This involuntary hospitality may become quite tiresome in practice. I remember one great Feasting. It was a ceremony for the dead. A Maharani had died, and we made her "praying-for-the-soul" budget, buying her sinlessness for 1,000 lives at a cost of Rs. 20,000. Part of the penalty was feeding Brahmins. Our budget provided for 3,000 guests: but it was not etiquette to shut the gates, and when 5,000 had been fed, my business soul did really take alarm.

"If the gates were shut by my order no ill-luck would betide the house, would it?" I asked of her of many years, who kept our abstract of right action. "Luck or ill-luck concern only the Believer" was her verdict . . . so my way was clear. In the courtyard great caldrons of food were steaming. Here was one stirring the rice and ever boiling more and yet more. On the veranda sat Brahmin cooks, cutting up red pumpkins or brown-green *brinjals*, slicing potatoes, grinding curry stuffs, dancing red-yellow grains of pulse in the winnowing fan. Other Brahmins ran to and fro, serving the food as it was made ready: all was orderly confusion, at which the women peeped from the third floor balcony.

They were the disciples of Priests at the expense of whose appetites we were buying merit, and they sat in rows, hungry and clamorous. Scarce could they be served fast enough.

"But how long will they sit there?" I asked of my old Dewan.

"Till they are fulfilled," was his delightful answer; and it gave me courage for the shutting of the gates.

It was but the day before that we had prayed for the soul of the Lady, at thirteen altars of holy Ganges mud. Four of these altars were arranged round a great central place of prayer, under an awning, to which were four "Gateways." At each gateway hung a looking-glass to hold the shadow of the spirit. . . . Beside the awning stood a wooden image of the dead, and to this was tethered a cow. So we bought for her blessings. This was also the purpose of the final ritual—gifts to Priests—silver vessels, beds with silken hangings, jewels of gold, and precious stones; . . . for the apostles of the order, whole travelling-kits—neat rolls of matting, drinking-gourds, umbrellas, begging-bowls. . . .

But, after all, it was in the Zenana that regret and longing were prettiest rendered. . . . In the hour of Ụnion (as we call the Twilight in Bengal), when the glories of the West had died into silence, and earth and sky were gray and still as life at the passing of a friend—she who was now Maharani—my ten-year-old Bride, crept out on to the landing of "the Inside" to sprinkle with holy water the place where soul and body parted, and to light the death-light of welcome.

"She will come back, and know that we have not forgotten."

It is interesting, the definite place in the scheme of life, allotted to women in a country where woman is of no account, except as handmaid to her lord man. I am always finding illustration of this truth. No spite, no resentment can rob individuals of the right to perform certain religious acts. The death-light, for instance, was the province of Boho-Rani, the daughter-in-law, the youngest in a household including three generations, and many collaterals. . . . But the most passionate love for the dead never suggested any variation of etiquette. The old Mother bent with grief, sisters, daughters sat huddled in the living-room, looking with hungry eyes at Boho, who alone could relieve the tension of that quiet-coloured hour by service.

Now it is the turn of one, now of another, the women know; there is no wrangling. . . . But a few days past there had been the Spring games, and the Festival of the Spring. The children-wives swung to and fro under the big tree in the women's courtyard. It was a pretty sight—the graceful little ladies in their bright draperies, clinging with their toes to the board (for they swing standing), holding to the ropes with tiny hands. . . . The sun peeped at them through the screen of leaves, and set on fire the rough-cut jewels at throat, at wrist, at anklet. To and fro, to and fro . . . so rhythmic was the motion, I found myself thinking of a field of grass, rippling in the wind. Some brides, too small for the exercise, were gravely swinging their dolls, and here was a "religious" fondling the baby Krishna in his cradle . . . but none of them played really: it was only—*Oberammergau*—how the god Krishna grown to manhood sported with the maidens; that was the reason given by all for the evening's gaiety.

Another day, with laughter and shy importance, the youngest Bride and Bridegroom were led to a place of prominence. It was their first Springtime since the marriage ceremony, and they sat side by side, bound together with silken cords; while the mother and grandmother threw at them little soft cushions of red powder, the same that is used in religious sacrifices for dusting the idol; with it is made the mark on the head of the Bride: perhaps the colour is symbolical, the women do not know, "it has always been so," they tell you.

And, as to the games—why it is Springtime, children should be merry, and the shy pelting with red pellets is Zenana merriment in italics. Next year, maybe, the Bride will be a mother, and such boisterousness will not become her. Let the children play while they may, and let the old Grand-dame pillow-fight with red powder cushions. Is she not nearer to the children in spirit than that grave-eyed Madan Mohun, of three Springtides, for instance, who is having his baby feed, in greedy solemnity. For is she not the wise woman of many years? and only the years can bring true youth and wisdom. Ignorance dies after decades of convention, of pain, of mistakes, and from the dead bulb springs this wonderful flower of youth and wisdom. The ignorance, the pain, the mistakes,—they had to be. Do they not make the fragrance of our Spring plant? The pity is when the original shrub knows no decay, when in the smug satiety of its evergreenness it journeys to no winter, and finds no aftermath of Spring.

On yet another day the youngest sister was chief lady. I found her sitting before a brass tray of glass bangles and silver ornaments. It was a first visit to her childhood's home since marriage, and her husband would break her old bangles and refit her. The Wise Woman says it is symbolical of the fact that even in her Parents' house she remains the possession of her husband. So he is admitted to the parental "Inside," and the women other than his wife, peep at the bangle-play from behind doors and curtains.

"What do Indian women do with their time?" how often I have been asked the question. Custom and religion make the day's programme—a woman's husband, and a woman's God, are occupation in themselves, and then there may be the children. The good Hindu will have her house of Gods, her private Chapel. Sometimes there is an image in it. I have known God-houses without any image. The name of the particular God it is right for her to worship will be whispered in her ear by the family Priest, and not even to her husband may she reveal the secret. But in her Chapel you will find most often in Bengal, an image either of the Baby God a-crawling, or of Kali, the Mother. In Krishna Chapels there will be a little crib, fashioned in these Western-

Eastern days like an English bedstead, with mosquito nets: and just as in the morning the devotee bathes and anoints the baby, leaving food beside it on the little altar, so at eventide she lights the nursery lamp and puts it to bed. . . . Is this Hinduism? I do not know. In practice it seems to me but the Mother-worship of the Child.

But in truth there is no one form or stage of Hinduism to be found in India, or, for the matter of that, in Bengal. . . . The great truths are eternal and prevail in every religion: yet all men are not capable of receiving the truth, and Hinduism recognizes this. In the actual worship of the idol are the illiterate and ignorant encouraged. "It would be sin to disclose to these the mysteries of a God not made with hands," so says the wisest of my wise women . . . "for he who has heard and hearkens not, and understands not, hath the greater sin." Yet that even a child may be capable of instruction she proves to you. I have seen many hundreds of babies under her roof, babies ranging from three to twelve years of age doing their morning *pooja.* It is "the worship of the possible" that she teaches them, "the worship of the Might-be."

At 9 o'clock they come hastening to the hour of prayer, like the birds and lizards of the Moslem legend: each little devotee, lips pursed in serious earnestness, is carrying her "basket of worship," and sits cross-legged to unpack it—an incense-burner, the bowl for Ganges water, flowers, bits of half-eaten fruit and vegetables, the sacrificial powder, often a remnant of some favourite saree, the Ganges mud with which to make her "idol"—all this she unpacks gravely, daintily, moulding her lump of clay into a cone. . . . Now she will make comparison with her neighbour, a little wistfully, perhaps, perhaps exultingly: often she shares her gifts. . . . Anything may be given to the God; the teaching here is to give what costs something, and when the *pooja* is over, the Pujari carries round a food-collecting plate for the animals within the gates, and the crows on the housetops. Now she is threading garlands of the sacred white jasmine, and the Priests have come for the chaunting.

The children sit in rows facing each other,

along the walls of the veranda. My Wisest of the Wise explains to me that the God who dwells within us is to be invited to inhabit that lump of mud (the clay on the potters' wheel), for His better worshipping by the children of men. So, the opening ceremony is a movement of the hands—the invocation! Each little worshipper sits wrapt before the God in the clay. . . . Now the Priest takes up the Sanskrit word, and the Babies chaunt it after him.

"Oh! Great God, bless us, forgive us, remain with us."

"Oh, Great God, I offer thee this incense, these flowers, this holy water," etc.

And the fingers are busy with the offering while every now and again "*Dhyan karo*" (meditate) will be the order: and five hundred pairs of Baby eyes are puckered into concentration and five hundred pairs of arms are tightly folded.

The earnest tension of the attitude moves one to tears. . . . Of what are they thinking? Oh! but of what?

"The worship of the Possible?"

That is the Wise Woman's thought, not theirs. I put it to her.

"Of what should they think," said she, "but of the whole duty of womanhood—to be a good wife: to omit no act of ceremonial Hinduism."

The sequence showed her wisdom. And being a good Hindu wife means fulfilling the duty of a Life-Bringer, thinking no evil of the lord who bears to you God's message of creation, counting his most temporal want as superior to your own most spiritual craving, making a religion of his smallest wish; and when the Gods, for your sins, take him from you, holding to his memory with prayer and fasting and self-suppression. . . . So we end, whence we set out *Devi—Goddess!*

V

THE SETTER-FAR OF IGNORANCE

I HAVE tried to indicate the women's attitude towards the man in India. His towards her is more difficult to determine—partly because she is not his whole existence, as he is hers; she is his occasional amusement, and always his slave and the physical element in the eventual saving of his soul, that complicated machinery which necessitates a son who will pay your material and spiritual debts. Comradeship, as we have seen, there can be little between orthodox Hindu husband and wife. Love we will not deny—these things are between soul and soul; show of affection would be insult in the presence of third persons; courtesy, in the thousand little ways required in the West, is shown rather by the woman to the man than by him to her. And, indeed, the very fact that he allows all this is proof of respect. To accept service is the compliment—and he respects her after his kind. But certainly he respects her. Does he not arrange that himself shall be her chief interest in life and her chief care and memory in death? Is she not allowed to be at once his "parasite and his chalice." But certainly he respects her. Her name may not be in the mouth of a man, even in the form of polite inquiry after her health: no strange man may see her face, and often he may not even hear her voice. Is it not her husband who guards her from contact with the outer world, from sight of God's most beautiful creation, from knowledge of the way he lives his life, or works, or plays?

But certainly he respects her. He eats the food she cooks for him, he gives her complete control of his household, and he sees that she lives up to his ideal of her place in the scheme of life.

She, too, has her ideal—the worship and service of her husband, and if he gives her opportunity to realize this, what more will she ask? When she is the mother of a son greater respect is hers, from the other women in the Zenana, and greater love and respect no doubt from her lord. Men do not like to be connected with a failure, and she has been successful, has justified her existence. The self-respect it gives the woman herself is most marked. She still is faithful slave to her husband, but she is an entity, a person, so far as that is possible in a Hindu Zenana; she can lift her head above the woman who taunted her, her heart above the fear of a rival. I have seen her parallel in the ugly duckling of the family who suddenly develops to the recognition of the outer world an unsuspected talent. We all know how she seems mysteriously and instantly to grow taller, smarter, more dignified; how she knows her own mind and has an opinion even in the regions remote from her special subject—whereas hitherto all had been vague discontent and vacillation. Both women are saying unconsciously in their hearts —"I am of use in the world," only I doubt whether, causes reversed, either would say it as triumphantly.

And, for a Hindu woman, "the best is yet to be." When she arrives at the dignity of Grandmother, ruling a household of daughters-in-law, she has indeed entered upon her kingdom. The son, who as infant first added to her stature, lavishes upon her in old age respect and affection which any woman might envy. Indeed, the relation of mother and son, even of widowed mother and son in India now, when her life is near its close, is the most beautiful perhaps of all Indian family relationships. She is respected, almost worshipped, as the Life-Bringer, and when she holds her grandson in her arms she is forgiven for the widowhood which for so long has been counted against her. At last she is loved as only those women are loved who have given, and given, and given all their lives seeking nothing in return.

I remember an old gray-headed Hindu saying to me, when we were discussing *Gurus*, "After all the true Guru in every house is the Mother; and are there not only three important things in the world—God, the Word of God, and the Guru, he who brings the Word?" . . .

Of the intellectual capacity of a woman a Hindu has a very poor opinion; but he will yield to, and even refer to, her about all matters of religion and—the kitchen.

It is the masculine attitude the world over.

And sometimes he will consult her about things she cannot possibly understand, from a superstitious belief that her virtue may give her insight. She is his toss of a penny.

It has often amused me to compare the men's and women's versions of some old-world story. It is extraordinarily enlightening. Once, in order to get a little nearer to the man's conception of a woman, I entrapped an orthodox friend of mine into telling me the story of the Ten-handed Durga. My friend was chewing betel-nut, which meant that he had dined, and was in genial mood, and clean white draperies. He sat cross-legged on a mat in a room all delicious cool open spaces. He leaned his elbow on a great white bolster. There were other bolsters and mats about the room, for it was his wont to sit here of an afternoon and receive visitors. It was his "Setting-far-ignorance" time, as he explained to me. One or two women sat beyond the mats; they were disciples of holy men, and allowed therefore to gather up the crumbs which fell from the table of the great philosopher. The scene pleased me. Every face in the room was worth study; some for the hall-mark of sainthood, many for the evidence of self-restraint and meditation; a few for an exactly contrary reason—the possibilities of a certain unholy strength, the best degraded to the worst.

There was a storm without, but the Setter-far of Ignorance heeded it not, even so much as to shut the windows, and the rain splashed in, and the lightning caught now one face, now another, now the pink garb of an ascetic, now the veiled form of a woman. . . . The thunder crashed, and ceased but to let in the noise of the street, with the tram of English civilization running under the windows.

My question about Durga set the heads wagging. It was close upon Durga Pooja time, and every Hindu would be provisioning his kitchen against guests, and adding to the house of Gods that image which presently he would carry down to the waters of forgetfulness. The question was popular.

"There are many versions of the story," said my friend. "You will have heard what the women say; the true tale is this. Not all the Gods could prevail against the powers of evil, so they united their several wills and energies, and the union of strength produced

Durga. She is energy or will—the beautiful Ten-handed—and she undertook to fight the demons.

"They came just in the form of beasts, and then of men; but both she slew. There lay at her feet the buffalo, typical of all that is coarse, and the lion, typical of all that is best in the animal world; and out of the slain beasts rose one in the likeness of a man, and him also she slew—victorious. It is in this form that the instructed worship her at Durga Pooja time."

Then I: "Expound the parable." And he: "See you not, the spiritual conquers the bestial and animal, thus gaining strength to conquer the human also. God conquers evil. And yes, I own it, the ultimate conquest of evil is by the agency of a woman, for the Creator so ordained it; she alone is capable of conquest *for others*—but they were the Gods and not the Goddesses who gave her the power to conquer. The Great God but accepted the service, the devotion in this matter of the woman, and so, has he not honoured her for all Eternity?"

"She alone is capable of conquest for

others"; "To accept service and devotion of any is the highest honour you can pay her." With that for key-note how many things are capable of understanding in the relation of Hindu man to Hindu woman!

"I see more still in your story," said one who sat by. "Does it mean also, perhaps, that only when we have renounced our wills can they be effectual for conquest, that when we give the best of ourselves to others, they afterwards, by these very means, bring back and lay at our feet that very thing we would ourselves have conquered and mastered?"

For of course the Gods had their part in Durga's victory. The Hindu remembers only that conquest, salvation may be bought for him by another. Suppose now the Hindu Mother to teach her son recognition of his part in that parable—that it is he who must cultivate the will and energy wherewith to gift the woman for conquest, possess himself of something worth giving—what a nation we should have!

But "Everything is in being through ignorance—when we are awake our dreams are false," was the only remark made by my friend to these heroics: and he yawned politely, and seemed to have lost all interest in the Ten-handed.

VI

THE KING OF DEATH

IT is in the villages, remote from railways that I have found the rarer God-tales, villages got at by long journeys of road and water, past lotus beds, the pink-white blossom growing waist high among leaves large as sun-hats; past groups of mat huts tottering against each other, past palm trees and green swamps of mosquitoes; past stretch of brown earth waiting patiently, face upturned, for the rain that comes not; once, past the quaintest requiem ever written in Nature. . . . It is a moment worth recall. A slow newly-constructed railway was making its weary way on a hot afternoon in June from mango-grove to river-bank and ferry steamer. It was the usual up-country landscape, one barely looked at it, till, suddenly a change—a great zone of sand, lying in *waves*, waves patterned like the ripple of water, and glistening—Earth's diamond tiara—in the fierce white light of the Sun-God. . . . A hot wind smote the face like a furnace-blast; the glare was a flame-red brand across the eyes . . . no relief anywhere, and yet, a strange sense of freedom in this sea of sand waves.

Under a bare tree of white thorns lay a small bundle of pink rags, a child with a shock head of hair, the only bit of life and colour anywhere it seemed at first. She lay quite still, on her back, motionless.

In the distance across the sand walked a woman, slowly, painfully; on her head was a water-pot, she walked away from the child, but every now and then she turned to look at the tree of white thorns. You knew what she sought . . . would she find it? and having found would she be in time?

The train crawled on to the river, and there was the woman ever walking away and away, and ever turning to look back; and the child under the shelter of a handful of thorn-needles still, so still, and the sun smiting on the gleaming sand. . . .

From the river in the growing dusk I saw

my diamond tiara changed to moonstones. . . . The great zone was now but a soft white sheen, a City of Light, and the minarets of some place of Saints towered above the battlements. "A very holy man lived there," they told me later. It is where holy men should live, it seemeth me, on the Sands of Time, their faces to that other fleeting Earth-force the River of Life. . . .

And it was travelling by ways such as these that finally I found myself in the canvas home of the wilderness, among people who had leisure to conserve the past, to remember. I sat with them, now on some spacious roof-tree, the sky for dome, now in some little box of a room, jealously guarded from light of day, or sight of man, or I went in and out with them to their Garden-houses, to their house of Gods, to the women's courtyard, which respect for hornets' lives had rendered dangerous to man! We were sitting in this same courtyard, my eye on the hornets' nest in the pipal tree, when "the slave of Kali" told me the tale of *Shoshti Devi*, the protector of women and children.

"It was a house-cat who first had knowledge of her," she said. "In a King's palace all the Queens were barren, and none could break the spell. So the cat chose her who oftenest thought upon her stomach's need, for the whispering of a secret."

"Go at midnight," said she, "and tend the turnips in the potter's field beyond the Gates." So, the youngest Queen went as she was bidden, and in six moons she had her desire." Shoshti Devi lives in trees, a different tree for every month; and the truly religious worship her in all these several forms—but it is enough if you make an image, just a head with a long red nose, and place it under one of the four most sacred trees. And, if you tie a rag to a branch as you go away, Shoshti Devi will look at it, and remember all about you and your prayer, what time you most may need her. . . . That was a wise cat. People unacquainted with the Indian temperament can have no conception of the pathological value of suggestions such as these. Be a woman never so ill, she comes back heartened and therefore better as an actual and visible fact for her visit to the Shoshti tree. Think of the faith it implies. No vision of the Goddess was vouchsafed her, no Priest comforted her, no wonder of music, no beauties of chancel or cloister drugged her soul or shampooed her senses: drawn by a legend not in itself necessary to salvation she but crawled to some dust-laden tree standing, may be, by a sun-baked highway. Perhaps she found there an image of *Shoshti*: perhaps not, it mattered nothing: and she tied to one of the branches her little prayer of rags, that was all. . . .

Such people should be easy to kill or to make alive. They are, and there lies the pity of it, in a world where you may die as well as live, be cursed as well as blessed. The Gods curse, but only through human agency. This is interesting since you may be blessed directly.

Knowledge on the subject of "sending devils" is the property of the Priesthood, Royal Fellows of the Society of Hellologists! but magic men and women, non-diplomaed and unlicensed also abound, and every dweller in town or village who has ever known or inherited a hate, has his own little stock of demonology for home consumption. It is my pride that on the one occasion when I was consciously operated upon, it was by the specialist. I had helped to secure protection for a child who had enemies, I was naturally therefore hated of these same. When back from her Estate, in the comparative civilization of my own little home, I got a much-thumbed message which had been thoughtfully left in my post-box.

"Twenty Priests learned in magic," so it ran, "are sending a devil into you." It was true. On the remote scene of thwarted vengeance, they were "making magic"—cursing a clay image made in my likeness, walking over every square inch of ground I had trod at the Palace, or in the Gardens, and—breathing curses.

My answer was a message, "To the Chief Priest among the twenty Priests most learned in magic, who sit in the Grove of Mangoes, at the Monkey Temple, in N . . . ., 'keep the Devil, till I come.'"

This was treated as a ribald tempting of the demon, and a man was sent to sit at my gate and curse me so that the flesh should wither from my bones, and my house be desolate. . . . But my household and my dear yellow "Chow," and my little gray mare, and my red-speckled *munias*, all the live things within my gates, did, with me, flourish exceedingly . . . and in a fortnight my twenty Priests withdrew their man, no doubt deciding that I had already a devil bigger than any at their command!

They were, alas! more successful with my little friend. First, they threw mustard before her as she walked, and she—sneezed. . . . "What would you?" It was Colman's mustard that you buy in yellow tins at the "Europe Shops." . . . But she sneezed—that meant a devil had entered, and the Priest spared not the picturesque in description of him. Then, one morning on her doorstep she found a little box—in it was a human thigh bone and three packets of powder—red, yellow, blue. This was a very potent curse, and she trembled exceedingly, so that she could not even name its meaning.[1]

[1] A knowledge of curses is a useful asset to Legal Advisers. I have known a serious family dispute composed on this wise. *A.* I could forgive everything but the bone under my bed, for this I will fight *B.* even till I am penniless. *Adviser* (Soothingly). Certainly, certainly—and now let's have the bone . . . which, produced, instead of being that powerful to curse, is merely a harmless leg-of-mutton bone! The way to peace is open.

But worst of all was the manner of cursing parallel to mine. There were at the moment great hopes of an heir to the Estate: the birth of a son would settle many political and domestic quarrels. The Priests chose the moment when the Mother's mind would be most open to suggestion, and cursed the thing that was to be! and it died.

So I have known another happening. A widow of fifteen had promised her Priest, at his desire, ornaments of a certain value for the Festival of Durga Pooja. But her Trustees did not sanction the expenditure. The Priest cursed her. She had two children—the youngest girl just eighteen months in age. The Priest was explicit in his curse—the Baby would die. I found my widow in an agony of grief. The child was her boy husband's last gift to her: and it was dying of pneumonia. . . . It was touch and go, but medical skill saved the little life, only the Mother's firm belief is that not science but the reconsidered decision of the Trustees, setting free her priest gifts, worked the cure.

And here I would mention one important article of belief in the Zenana. It is that not only a man himself but that which he owns or loves or values may be affected by magic. "So-and-so has put a curse upon your cattle," will be a message followed by mysterious deaths, not to be accounted for by poison. The form of the message varies—it may be sent in words, it may be sent like the thigh bone or the mustard, in kind—that is of small moment, the result is always the same.

My Wisest of the Wise, asked for explanation, is politely full of wonder that I should wish for explanation of such things. "Is it possible that I doubt? If these things were capable of understanding would they be worth a thought? Is not the supernatural of necessity beyond reason? Would you plough the stars with bullocks? Has anything any existence at all, except in our belief? All we are or seem is a dream. Those who doubt and argue would seek to dream waking; and they lose so all the pleasing restfulness of sleep."

Then musingly, she turned to me with her rare smile. "Once, I also doubted. I was then of few years, and the questionings which belong to the changing part of me were many. I was in Benares, and I said to a holy man there, who is of one fellowship with me: 'This thing—cursing—is of the evil one. Do not practise it. Besides I do not believe you can curse. I believe it is only magic, like the gypsy folk do use. And he: 'Nay, Mother, I do it in the name of the Writings—try me.' And I wished to test this thing, but because I had said it was wrong, I could not then consent. Yet on the third day I said: 'Well, if you can work a curse in a good cause . . . I will be witness.'

"The Gods sent the occasion. A poor man, threader of flowers for the neck of a sacred bull in a rich man's temple, came to me the next day. He and his family were starving. The rich man had out of caprice dismissed them. My holy man turned to me.

"'This is the occasion of your seeking, Mother,' he said. 'That rich man is known to me. I will hurt him—but not much—for this poor man's sake.'"

She smiled again whimsically. "I was in the body—what would you? It was wrong: but I consented.

"So the holy man sent for a little dust from off the feet of the rich man, and with the help of this, and some earth and flour, he made an image, saying *mantras* the while; but the most powerful mantras said he over five nails lying in the bottom of a pot.

"'Now,' he said, 'the curse is ready; but first go and see the rich man. Is he well? bring me news.'

"So I went, even as I was bid, and I sat in the courtyard and saw for mine own self that he was well, and vaunting himself in his health and riches.

"It was dusk when I returned and made my report. 'Then here begins the magic,' said the holy man; and taking one of the nails he had cursed, he drove it with many more curses into the knee of the image.

"'A little curse,' he said, 'only a little curse in a good cause: but he shall feel it.'

"And I ran back to the great house and found all in confusion—servants running for doctors, Priests reciting prayers. . . . 'The Master was sick unto death,' they told me. We waited that night; and in the dawn hour, I, being holy myself and privileged, went to the rich man and told him as he lay in agony, that to my mind, not the doctor, but expiation would cure him.

"'What!' he said, startled, for his sins I think were not few, 'must I bear penalty in this life, when I am willing to carry my burden in the next.' 'Oh! a small matter,' I suggested; 'something easy of expiation. Think —a wrong perhaps to some private or Temple servant.' But he remembered nothing. So I, pretending I had seen the thing in a dream, told him, and instantly the threader of garlands was sent for and honoured with gifts and feastings. When the holy man heard of this he took the nail from the rich man's knee and he recovered immediately. . . . Yes, I believe in curses. But they are not good, they belong to the things of the body."

"*Sitting dharna*" is the Curse Coercive. I thought the practice extinct, till last year I found a half-mad thing mechanically telling his beads in a Raj courtyard of my acquaintance, as he sat beside the image of Ganesh the luck-bringer, under the pipal tree where lay the offerings of red and yellow flowers and sacred grass-tufts. It was midday and he sat bareheaded in the sun, unkempt, unshaven, blear-eyed.

So had he sat a fortnight, touching neither

food nor drink. The lady of the house disputed a debt claimed by him in the name of an ancestor. She bade him sue, but he, wise man, preferred this method. At the moment he was only just alive, and his wits seemed to have preceded him to the new genesis. We called him back, with kind words and chinking of money under the trunk of the Luck-Bringer himself. It was the money I think that reached him on the Border Land. He laughed for joy and wept many salt tears into his first spare meal of rice and watery pulse; but the family borrowed more money to make a great feast because the house was saved from a Curse!

Another variety of compelling your desire is the burning of a cow or an old woman. While, for a woman, the simplest way is the time-honoured custom of sulking. Early Indian domestic architecture provides for this. There was always a sulking-room in the "Inside" (compare *boudoir*), and here sat the woman who insisted on her own way; and here no doubt came husband or father with gift of shawl or toe-ring to release her. . . .

My wise ones tell me many stories as we sit on the roof in the hour between the Twilights. But the story of my Wisest one herself is one of my favourites. You must know that she is a very holy woman indeed. At her birth, so many years ago that her devotees bring you data to prove her a hundred years old, it was prophesied that she would be "a religious," and her Father built her a Shrine, and taught her things which only Priests may know. She can perform every *jog*, and can read one's thoughts in any language. Her face is the face of her who has attained, and her dignity and self-poise I have nowhere seen surpassed. She dresses oddly—the sex of the devotee must not be proclaimed—in the nether garments of a man, *i.e.*, loose white drapery about the legs, and a long coat. Her hair is worn in coils on the top of her head, and round her neck hang sacred beads, and Kali's necklet of skulls in gold and enamel work. To her the symbol is not gruesome. Kali, she will tell you, was the power of God, the "Energy of the Gods," and the heads represent the Giants of wickedness whom she has slain.

She is extraordinary in her dealings with people, so quick to discern true from false; so fearless in her denunciation of hypocrisy, withal that she is never aught but courteous. I love sitting beside her when pilgrims come, pilgrims from all parts of India who fall at her feet and pass on to other shrines, or linger in the outer courtyard on the chance of a word; the meaning of a text, some family or caste difficulty, advice as to the moment's physical or worldly need, all are brought to her; for she shuts out nothing, and is a dear *shrewd* Saint about business other than her own. I have known her wave off a pilgrim—"She would not insult her feet" was the reason given. She seemed to gather all that mattered about this type of person in a single glance. To one who came in curiosity pure and simple, though he pretended interest in some Sanskrit text, she said, quietly looking him in the eyes while he fumbled over his unveracities: "No! you shall not hear whence I came, nor anything about me." But to another more sincere, though equally curious, she said—he had spoken no question—"I come from a land where women ride and men wage war."

In 1857 she was already a famous Sanskritist, so powerful that her influence, purely religious, was mistaken for political. She was suspected of collusion with Khande Rao Peishwa, and a guard of soldiers was stationed round her cell and Temple. When the country settled down, she wandered to the different places of pilgrimage all over India, meditating and buying merit. Everywhere had she been, everywhere that is holy, and as an old woman, eyes dim with prayer, throat drawn with fasting, she has settled in Bengal and devotes herself to the religious education of her community. "I have spent a lifetime in prayer: now I am ready to work," she explains. But the praying is not over.

From 5 to 9 of a morning, she shuts herself away in her House of Gods, and no one dare disturb her. Here in India, where shrines are many, and there is no false shame about entering and praying—doors wide—nay, where the Godling sits by the wayside, and where it is a common thing to see a woman stand on a highway, head against some outer wall of a Temple—the moment's contact a prayer, or bowing to the Earth on some crowded pavement—it is curious that not one of her devotees or friends has any knowledge of what is within her House of Gods—whether it is empty or has the whole panthology. Yet all alike—alien in faith, disciple, or visiting devotee—have seen her face as she leaves that house after her communings with eternity; and well—is there not a story of the Mount of Transfiguration?

So, she cured herself of a serious illness during which, thinking it (perhaps meaning it) to be her last, she had summoned to her side by some telepathic power the faithful from all parts of North India. I say "meaning," because I am forced to believe that the Indian woman who has her will in training can die at will: more rarely she can live at will. Probably the latter is the rarer because, poor thing, she has so much more incentive to die than to live.

Well, this time my Wisest of the Wise had elected to live after all. Her choice was not incompatible with her faith in a God who held the keys of Life and Death. It was only that, being given free will, it was within her power to steal the key of the House of Death.

"Has one ever stolen the key of the House of Life?" I asked.

"I know of none such," was the cautious answer of wisdom.

Then I—"Talk to me, Mother, of Life and Death. What is Life?"

And she—"A dream in the heart of a dream. . . . It is as if one should sleep, and sleeping dream that he was dead. That dream within a dream is this, that men call Life."

"And Death?"

"To-morrow's dream. The next-door house. God's tenant am I in this house in which you find me. But agreement I have none. God will tell me to quit, nor give me notice. Death is but the house I next inhabit. There will be other houses after that." Death, it would seem, is but a change of house, we have failed to repair the present tenement, or it is too small for us, or our neighbourhood is unsuitable, so we are given the chance of another, and after that, perchance, yet another and another, through all the lives appointed to us. But our personalities remain. We can never sink those.

Once again, she talked of Death as "the Innermost Dream—but we shall wake." "The end of the Death dream is only sleep, that is Life: when we wake from life, it is to Life Eternal."

"And what is that?"

"Rest—in the perfect attainment of all truth, of all knowledge and of all reality."

The body, I gather, is degradation to the soul. Any "house" is in a measure degradation and belongs to the state of progress. Some day we shall be free of all houses. We shall lose ourselves in the Great Soul. That is the final "Twilight"—the time of Union for each individual soul.

"Then shall there be no more Death." . . .

She ceased speaking, my Wisest of the Wise, and silence fell between us as we looked together at the dying Sun.

Oh! the gray and silver gray on the water. Oh! the gold, limpid, liquid, lambent gold in the sky and on the water. . . .

"And the King of Death is but the first Sunset." . . .

P.S.—Since the above was written, my Wisest of the Wise has arrived at her Sunset hour. Her going was very beautiful and very simple: shortly before her time was come, she left the Town where she dwelt, for the holy city of Death. She was no worse and no better than she had been any day the year and more, but she knew, apparently. Then, one morning, she said quite calmly to her disciples, after the ceremonial bath and *pooja*, "This is the last time I shall worship in this house" (her body); "now, waste no time in regret, let us talk the things we should be sorry to have left unsaid." . . . And all that day the faithful gathered about her, and she expounded the scriptures with an insight unequalled even by herself. She ate nothing—"Why prop up the house that is tumbling?"

At night she asked to be taken down to the Sacred River—a Hindu dies with her feet in the water; and there she sat among her friends on the stone steps of the Ghat, claiming no support, no physical comfort, now silent, now setting afloat some beautiful thought in words that will always live for those who loved her . . . and then just in the gray mystery of the dawn hour, "It is right," she said, and fell back. . . . They put her into a boat and took her across to the Ghat of the Soul's departure, and here they slipped her gently into the Stream . . . for that is all the burial service for one who is holy.

Later, her disciples came to me with faces radiant. "She has attained," they said. "Yes!" said the Holy Man, Truth-named, "she has attained in that she elected not to attain;" and then they told me that, sitting that night of stars and dark spaces by the River of Death, one had said to her: "You are blessed; you have attained." And she made answer: "Nay! it was given me to attain; but I put it aside, desiring re-birth once more for the sake of the work, to which I have put my hand, here among you."

"And a man's future is even as his desires. That is true truth, Miss Sahib!" concluded the Wise man, Truth-named.

VII

THE WISE MAN—"TRUTH-NAMED"

IT was at the house of my Wise Woman that first I saw him. He wore a straight long robe, the colour of the pilgrim flag, or of the inner lining of the fruit of knowledge when you break through the sheath in which it shelters from the world.

About his head were wound fold on fold of muslin of the same mystic hue, and the way of winding, and his speech, bewrayed him of the Punjab.

But as I have said, you must never locate the holy. He walked with head erect, straight as an arrow, nor receiving nor giving salutation to any; and he came to me where I stood talking to my Wisest of the Wise, and "When," said he, "may I come to talk with the Miss Sahib of the big-little things?" And I: "How know you that I like to talk of these things? and what are they?"

"I know; the Miss Sahib knows. When may I come?"

So we found a convenient season; and he, the free, made of himself for the sake of removing ignorance, a slave of time, coming punctually Sunday after Sunday to talk the big-little things, "Life and Death," and "Whence we come," and "Whither we are bound."

With eyes screwed together in earnestness, one finger on the tip of his nose as he meditated, he would talk hour after hour; nor did he discourage discussion, he begged it. It was one way he said of teaching us to know ourselves. "And how shall we know God until we know ourselves?" "Be self-knowers. God is within, and it is the God in us that seeks to find God." . . . "God! by what sign shall we know Him? how conceive? Imagine a world without space or place or time or anything created. Imagine only light and light and light, everywhere pulsing, throbbing. . . . From the beginning was that, and only that, and that was God. But with God exists the Power and Mercy of God, not separately, but as closely allied as sweetness to sugar, as the scent of the rose to the rose, as the colour of a flower to the flower. . . . Men talk of one God as if there could be two or three. There 's just God—the All-pervading, the Essence of Being, the heart of the heart of Beauty, the great first Flame which lights every flame that leaps into life. . . . Light and light and light, brilliance at the soul of brilliance . . . the God-spark in every soul, in everything created . . . only by recognizing this shall we recognize God, there is no other way.

". . . Yes! the windows of the soul get dimmed and the flame gives no light. Is that the fault of the flame? Clean the windows of the soul; such work is allowed to man, such only, not his to create Light, *that* was and is from Eternity.

"One day all the several sparks of light will go back to the Great Central Light whence they came, the soul will find God. . . . What need to make haste? What need to fret? Every soul must find God at long last . . . light will return to Light."

In countries loved of the Buddha one sees by the roadside a little shrub with white leaves among the green. The Buddha passed that way, is the legend, and the shrub has kept memory of the passing. I have sometimes thought that so among the leafy professions of mankind there are some white souls that keep the memory of the passing of the Great God. The "Truth-Named" is one such.

I remember on one occasion thanking him when he had said things which gave food for thought.

"Huh!" he said, "Miss Sahib, that was not yet talk of God. I did but try to make a clearing in the jungle where we might sit down and meditate about these things." Another day he said: "There are three diseases in the world—*Actual Sin*" (the breaking of what we call commandments), "this disease can be cured by good works; *Restlessness*, to be cured by meditation; and *Joylessness*, to be cured by making occasion to give joy to others. The mark of a true religion is Joy."

Referring to the first cure, I said: "Then you believe in the efficacy of good works, oh! Truth-Named Singh." And he said: "Good works are fetters, fetters of gold, but still fetters."

* * * * *

When the Datura tree hung out its burden of bells, and the pilgrim season had begun, he came to me with as much excitement as his calm abstraction from all emotion permitted. And, "There is a *Lat* (Lord) Swami," he said, "sitting in a grove at Dum Dum. Would the Miss Sahib like to talk with him?"

"Is he holy?" I asked.

"I know him not, but he is called a *Lat* Swami, he should be so. He has been teaching the people of the farther England (America) about God and the one religion, it is said, and he has many disciples in every country. Besides, he speaks the language of the Miss Sahib's friend (English), and it is a chance for the Miss Sahib's friend to question in her own tongue, as she cannot me." . . .

So we went, and the first time lost our way. We met strolling minstrels and were offered seats at wedding feasts, and fighting rams for our diversion, but no Swami sitting by his Lake of Lotuses.

Our Wise Man was distressed: "I gave my word you would come. Even by mistake we cannot break a word, it is damage to Sainthood"—one's own he meant. "Make a speedy occasion to remove the disease of this error. I myself will conduct you."

But no! he would not arrange the train by which we were to go. "Shall I who am free, compel any to be slaves to time? Come when you will, I will sit at the Station all day." It was late afternoon when we could make the expedition but the "Truth-Named" was there. He had awaited us since morning, meditating undisturbed by the bustle of a Railway Station. We were soon in the suburbs among palm-trees, and rank undergrowth, and we found the *Lat Swami* clad in yellow-silk robes, sitting cross-legged in a grove of mango-trees, beside a bed of white lotuses. His face did not appeal, but that we mused, might be prejudice.

"Ask him the big-little questions," prompted our Wise Man—himself retiring deferentially to the level of the least of the Lat Swami's disciples. And we asked, only to hear in pompous English, "I refer you to my book, which has been well reviewed by the 'Daily Mail.' My Disciple will explain." And before our gasp of astonishment had spent itself, came the disciple, a follower from that "farther England" who, grovelling before the Master, produced the book.

But we were busy inventing excuse for flight. Silence, as we walked away. Then said our Truth-Named, tolerant humour in his eyes, "So the Miss Sahib's Friend, and the Miss Sahib liked not that Holy Man?"

"*No!*" I said, "we did not." Pause—then, "I am glad the Miss Sahib's Friend, and the Miss Sahib did not like that Holy Man. I am glad that they gave not their discrimination a sickness by liking him."

"But you took us!"

"How could I know? Besides, in a garden one should smell every flower. . . . To me it seemeth that the foolish ones of the Farther England have robbed him of his virtue by their admiration and praises. It is ever so. Of virtue do women rob even the holy. Once that Swami had excuse for knowledge."

"What is the name of her whom he called Disciple?"

"How can I know? Foolish one—what need for other name?"

On the way back we had proof of our Wise Man's reality of religion. He would not travel in our carriage behind the "fire horse," politely went next door: but just as the train was about to move we saw him literally kicked out by some non-Indian, masquerading as a gentleman.

The poor old "Truth-Named" found room elsewhere, and nothing could be done till we arrived at our destination, when we waited for him to apologize and atone for the unknown.

"Huh," he said, "*that*, that was nothing. Forget it, Miss Sahib. It is not. It could not hurt me, since I did not resent it." . . . "His mind carried not fruit of ignorance," as he said on another occasion. Even so, in his simplicity has he often enunciated the greatest of truths.

I have talked in a book of women of Holy Men, for priests and women are allies the world over, and in India, particularly is the influence noticeable. A priest is often the only man with whom a Purdahnashin may talk, before whom she may appear unveiled: and, as I have said before, there is a secret, albeit about things religious, between wife and priest to which even the woman's husband may not be party. Not backward has the Priesthood been in availing itself of its privileges. Where his learning is not likely to attract, the man of ashes has an inheritance of superstition to which no woman is proof, and from which there can be no appeal.

The "Truth-Named" is fearless in denunciation of the ash-smeared and degraded type of Priest. "In the golden age the only Priest was Prayer. If we would only study ourselves, travel in the unknown country of our minds and souls and personalities, we should need no Guru, save God. Priests, of all religions, keep men's eyes bandaged that they should not see except through the Priest: but the written word and the book of ourselves is open to all."

"There is but one religion—the service of man and personal holiness by realization of God. No need for rules of conduct, for commandments. Realize God and even the desire to transgress is slain. But realize God and the place even of sin in the scheme of the world will be clear. There is nothing which is which is outside God. Yes—this is a hard doctrine, to be learnt only by sitting aloof from men, sitting in a place of green trees, in solitudes where blow the winds of God, fresh and pure."

Perhaps one reason of the ascendency of the Priesthood was that at one time the priests were the moneylenders of the Community. We know this was so even as late as the eighteenth century. Say a man wished to borrow £3: he went to the Faqir who put the sum into his hand in the presence of witnesses, but about 15*s*. had to be returned to himself as a present. Interest was never less than 12 per cent. and the lender kept a watch-dog at the expense of the borrower, to see that he did not run away! So the poor wretch seldom got more than half the sum he borrowed, while, to compel repayment, children were often sold, and most cruelly tortured.

It is curious to recall in this connection the old Sanskritic tale of the learner who went to the Sage to ask what might be the best penance for deeds of evil.

"Gifts of Cows, of land, and especially of gold to Brahmins."

"Why specially gold?" "The purifying power of gold, Oh! Purusurama," was the answer, "is very great. They who bestow it, bestow the Gods."

"How so?" said the obstinate Learner.

"Know, oh! Hero, that *Agni* (fire) comprehends all the Gods, and gold is of the essence of Agni."

Women Priestesses there are; but not as a regular institution of the Purdah. If it is right to conclude that the system of seclusion is encouraged and italicized by the Priests in order to preserve the man's monopoly, the reason will be obvious.

Also it would seem as though except as a religious elect before or from birth, or remarkable for peculiar learning, like my Holiness, the Priestess chooses the humbler position of the service of a Guru, leaving guidance to her male counterpart. Some act procurator in positions not possible of relation; but there must be exceptions, and one charming young Priestess at least have I known who owed her attractions neither to the sacred learning nor to prophecy. She was from the North country, and appeared suddenly one pilgrim season in the vicinity of Nasik, in Western India. Tall and beautiful, of commanding presence, clad in shell-pink draperies; a close-cropped head, discoloured to a brilliant copper by the fumes of the opium fire—such was the figure that stood, pilgrim flag in hand, by the roadside, asking protection of a passing stranger. Remarkable to look upon she would have been in any costume, but thus, against the glow of a low sun-setting, she was arresting.

And her story? full of humour and pathos. She and a younger Brother, orphaned early in life, were left to the care of an Uncle. The property was the Brother's with reversion to herself. The Brother died while still a child; helped out of life, she conceived when old enough to understand these things, and the property was hers and she bride-elect to her cousin. She had loved her Brother passionately—Oh! you saw that, in her eyes and in the picture she left with you of her attempts to push Death away from the threshold. "Stroke the brindled cow," was the last prescription of the old Priestess, who sat in the near-by forest: and the child brought in the old cow to the neglected bedside. Then, in a frenzy, she ran to the old Priestess: "Cut off my hair"—she was but ten years old—"and initiate me. It will, maybe, please the Gods, and spare the life." And the Priestess, alleged seller of God-favours, initiated the child, being not unaware of her position and prospects.

But when the beloved Brother died, and the Uncle sought to recover the child, she refused to come, nor could she now as initiated Priestess be bride to the cousin. So a bribe to the opium eater procured silence, and the disciple her freedom.

It was a wandering life—now grove, now cave, now hill camping-ground—the little Priestess sitting over the opium fire, her head on a prayer-stick, meditating—her instructress raking in the offerings. A prayer-stick is shaped so—**T**: and the head lies on the arm stretched across the bar, while the fumes of the opium fire produce drowsiness. But the life of prayer and meditation, in the name of her Brother, became very real to the Baby Priestess: and as she grew, and her Old-Woman-Guru used her to attract devotees to the Shrine, there was many a tussle between righteousness and unrighteousness, till policy suggested the Child's sanctity as the more lasting bait.

She must have been about twenty when they made the pilgrimage to Nasik; and here the old woman met her own one-time Guru, and he claimed the prayer-stick of the beautiful grand-disciple as a talisman. Perhaps he claimed more, we were not told; but the rupture on refusal brought her to that wayside throwing of herself on the mercy of a stranger. . . . She was wonderfully adaptive to the demands of civilization, cast away her opium pipe, and even struggled bravely with forgotten memories of reading and writing; but she loved best to sit huddled up in the dusk and tell stories of her wanderings. What stories they were!

"In every house a Father, in every house a Mother"—a great phrase with her; and soon, the wander spirit proved too much for her. The road called her, and she went—comet-like. This was many years ago; but I still hope to come upon the copper-headed owner of the prayer-stick.

Once I thought I had found her at a place of pilgrimage in company with a holy woman who had gained her reputation for sanctity in a way unusual. She was an untaught Mathematician, sat at the mouth of a cave drawing geometrical figures in the sand, and spelling out for herself the problems which the world of books has dedicated to other names than hers. The pilgrims thought the triangles and parabolas magic, and would wag wise heads over the Mathematician at work; quite content if after the cabalistic musings which had nothing to do with their goods and ills she announced to the inquirer that there would be a good harvest, or that his son would die and his enemy be degraded in rebirth.

But if it were indeed my Comet whose copper head hung over a prayer-stick behind the Mathematician, I got not opportunity for speech or sight. Yet, I am thinking that some day, when the sun is low, that column of burnished light will wait for me once more beside the Pilgrim's way.

VIII

THE NASAL TEST

A STUDY OF CASTE

CASTE in its origin was merely a guide to marriage, *i.e.*, a man was distinguished from his fellow-men simply in order to determine into what families a woman might or might not marry.

Moreover, a "County" family was known by the width of its nose, caste varying inversely as the width. For the only question with which caste dealt in the long ago, was: Are you an Aryan or are you a Dravidian?

There were later stages, influenced, who can say, by what motives? providing, how know we now, for what momentary need? serving, who shall tell us, what personal spites or conveniences? and caste came finally to denote not only a man's place on the social ladder, but his privileges in a spiritual kingdom and his value in a professional market.

It is a little difficult to explain because there is, I think, no exact parallel in the institutions of the West. It is a combination of several determining causes of exclusiveness—the social Western conception of the right instinct and the appropriate culture, the interests of labour as represented by trade-guildism, and the Judaic idea of a chosen people as something peculiarly the care of a God who nevertheless made all the world.

And, at the present day, the social and economic distinctions are merged in the religious, so that the feeling, as we find it, is of a barrier placed by God, not man. Is it not exactly otherwise in the nearest parallel afforded by the West? Your neighbour may, in Church, I take it, assume the privileges of an equal; in the Park he may not. The Hindu high-caste man might joke and laugh with his inferior in the Park; but he will not go to Church with him, *i.e.*, he will not eat with him because this is a religious act, and he will not "pray" with him in the sense of admitting him to certain mysteries of the religion, or the performance of certain sacrifices. Again, caste implies breeding, only relatively. Indeed, even the lowest person in the scale of life will talk of his caste. "I am of the caste of the sweeper," he will say quite proudly; and he has further been known to say: "I am of the caste of—the Outcast"; because he knows of some one who will do what is tabooed even to him. Caste—that is—denotes a man's place on the ladder of life, but not of necessity his place on any one rung rather than another. In this sense, it is a mere label.

Further, we must remember that with Caste as a rule—*nascitur non fit*. There have been known people who used a semblance of tribal name to climb into a caste above their own; or again, take the "Eaters-in-relief-kitchens," a caste in Orissa made, we are told, of those who lost their original caste by accepting relief in famine time; and there are at our doors others, who by persistent self-restraint and imitation of the customs of a higher caste pass by courtesy for such; but these do not deceive the elect into intermarriage. A man may buy himself salvation, a higher place in the world to come by his spiritual re-genesis. There is no bribe of whatever kind which in this world, will put him on to even the very next rung of that ladder of Caste.

Now, is it clear that with all this machinery of exclusiveness there is no condemnation one of another? If I am of the highest caste, in this genesis, sitting on the top step of our socio-religious ladder, and you, say, on the fourth, I must of necessity exclude you from "bread and water." That rule our religion, which is greater than either of us, has made; but that does not mean that I will not associate myself with you in other ways. True, I would not let my Zenana visit yours—my women are part of my religion—but you and I might play together, buy and sell together, work together, travel together. . . .

And yet, again, this contamination against which I am bound to guard myself is ceremonial not moral. It is not because you would teach me to swear or lie or thieve that I cannot dine at your table, but because drinking water at your hands, and eating what has been cooked at your fire, is within the canonical "Thou shalt not." The odd thing is that until English education brought other ideas to the country, no one resented his place in life. "Why kick against the inevitable?" he would argue. "I shall come again; who knows but that in my next genesis I might not myself be sitting on that topmost step?" All is in a man's own hands—he will reap hereafter, as he sows now this minute. . . .

And Hindu women? How has caste affected them? We have seen that it was invented primarily for their benefit, for though a man might marry beneath him, no woman was allowed like liberty. The natural result of this arrangement was that there were too few men to go round in the higher castes; and in a scheme of life and after life which has no room or use for spinsters, the only resource was to marry them off as quickly as possible, whence, in the opinion of some, infant marriage, though the instinct of self-preservation against Mahommedan raids must have done something.

Of course, no woman realizes this, and the reason she will give you for Baby marriages is that a Father's class of Heaven depends on the age at which his daughter was married. If she is settled between three and five he goes to a first-class heaven, if between five and eight to a second class, eight and eleven to a third class—after that to hells, only to hells! For herself she is content with the most detailed and minute table of procedure, nor questions how it was made. She knows far better than any man the difference between + A and − A. She will tell you also quaint exceptions to the God-rules. "You may stand by So-and-so when she is cooking a dish of green (but not red) pulse, and never *never* when she is cooking rice. It would all have to be thrown away, it and the vessels, even if the shadow of a shadow fell across it." In South India I have heard tell of a caste of Brahmins so strict that no lower caste may come within thirty yards of its elect; and when the high-caste woman walks abroad, she has a fore-runner clearing the way before her face.

Again, with some castes not only must you, being alien or of a lower caste, not touch their water or water vessels, but you must not enter the room which holds the drinking-water. If you do, the water is defiled. They have too good manners to tell you this. It may be their last drop of water in a drought, nevertheless, when you have gone away, the water is faithfully rejected. Nor, again, may they drink water even at the hands of the elect if the alien or outer-brother is in the room.

Different civilizations, different notions of cleanliness. The point seems to be to learn each other's aversions and respect them. The Hindu is horrified at the use of tooth-brushes. "What! use the same brush twice?" She herself uses a twig of the *Neem* tree, no fatter than her own smallest finger, and of course there is a fresh twig for each using. Again, at the use of tubs, "You go dirty into the water from which you expect to come out clean," she exclaims. You refer gently to the bathing in the Ganges. "Ah, but that is different," she will answer, "that is holy water, however apparently impure, however apparently contaminated, it is holy." Her reasoning explains what hitherto puzzled me —how little particular the Hindu is about the intrinsic cleanliness of water, despite her belief in sacred streams. The Founders of the religion, knowing the value of water in a hot country, called it sacred, no doubt in order to keep it clean. Their thought was, "It is sacred, do not defile it." The modern Hindu says, "It is sacred—even the thing that most defiles, cannot defile it."

The same Hindu who will bathe before touching the sacred basil, will be absolutely indifferent as to the water in which she bathes. If it is a sacred river, a sacred tank, it may be thick as pea soup with impurities. That is no matter. . . . Again, another incongruity. The eating of the flesh of the cow revolts a Hindu—you do not realize how strongly till it is something other than yourself—as a dog, suspected of a meat diet, who sniffs at them; and yet the sacrifice of goats at Kalighat, for instance, cannot be seen unmoved by the most inveterate eater of flesh.

The fact is, that with the Hindu the root of all aversion is traditional religion, and this it is which overlays the ordinary aversions of instinct or culture. At the present day purely arbitrary, too, seems the table of clean and unclean, though, as in all religions, no doubt it had its one-time significance. In an agricultural country the cow was a useful animal. If you wished preservation, the only way was to declare it sacred. The religious sanction appeals most strongly to peoples in their infancy, and in India we find a nation which still keeps its nursery rules, so to speak. . . . And, as is proper, the women know far more about these rules than do the men. A Hindu will often say, appealed to on this point or that of religious custom or religion: "I do not know, but information may be had in *the Inside.*" One such Inside produced the fact that the sanctity peculiar to the Ganges applies to one town at least, to Puri by the Sea. As the Ganges receives all castes—in death, so does Puri—in life.

Here such holiness does the very fact of residence give, that it over-rides distinctions. A Brahmin would eat at the hand of a sweeper in Puri, would eat and keep his caste. In theory, of course, a man should eat at the hand of a sweeper anywhere, a sweeper, say, turned *Sanyasi* (a world-renouncer or holy man); but my same information adds as rider that no Sweeper, even in Puri, would dream of thrusting himself on a Brahmin.

I referred the point to my Wisest of the Wise. "It is true," she said, "and only the holiest Brahmin, he who has got so far past the trammels of his body as not, say, to be conscious of even heat or cold—for caste is only a distinction of this body—only such a man would say to the Sweeper, 'Come, friend, the God in you and the God in me is one: let me eat at your hands,'—and such an one could take no sin eating with the Sweeper. But as long as you are conscious of repulsion, aversion, there is sin in disregarding it—sin which will affect the after-genesis, which will annul a life-time of merit."

This same penalty, loss of caste, is the reason for what has been called in official documents "enforced widowhood." The Priests attached excommunication to re-marriage. And since, as we have seen, things social and things religious overlap in Hinduism, the Priests had the opportunity of banning in both ways. No more invitations to caste dinners, as well as no more visits to the Temple, to sacred Tanks and Wells and Bathing Ghats, for the excommunicated. Few women and fewer men will face excommunication of this type, and one reads with amusement of the ardent reformer who, before proposing marriage to a charming widow of his acquaintance, wrote a hundred notes to friends and acquaintances, "Will you dine with me if I marry So-and-so?" There were not fifty righteous found willing, even on paper! But in truth the number of those who wish or would countenance re-marriage is very small. The feeling of the orthodox about marriage is this: It is a Gift—the gift by a Parent of a daughter to a husband. The Gift must be a *first* Gift, no one must have had earlier use of it, no one must even have had earlier chance of longing for it. You must be certain the possession is your very own—wherefore the giving in infancy. Wherefore again, even if you died after mere symbolic and before actual possession of your gift, the Gift was nevertheless yours. . . . Infant widowhood. How can it be given again—that Gift? If it would be sin in infancy, it would be worse sin later on. And the woman's reasoning is of the same class. The best believe in the sacrament of marriage: they worship their husbands as the life-force: for his using or abusing, his pleasure or neglect they exist. He being gone, what is there? In the old days there was suttee, and who shall say but that the moral strength it represented did not make for something in the national consciousness? No one ever enforced widowhood. No one enforced suttee: no one to-day can really restrain suttee. One old test was putting your smallest finger into the fire and burning it to the bone: if you could stand that, unflinching, you were worthy to be suttee. Another was stirring boiling hot rice with your bare hand. I know a woman whose proudest memory is that some Great-Aunt or Grandmother stood the test.

Of course misuse of the practice crept in. Some women became suttee because it was expected of them. What tragedies there must have been! How the other women must have whispered: "Will she be suttee? Oh! will she?" or, "She surely will be suttee!" And in each case it would have determined the undetermined. Again, one can imagine the woman who did not love suffering suttee in expiation, or in terror at her own gladness of release; or she who was not loved enough seeking it in pride or hunger of heart. Oh! the tragedies in that handful of ashes on the suttee stone. Then, again, there would be the Priest-made suttees, an increasing number as the years carried life further and further from the original ideal.

But, as I said above, the real suttee was never compelled, nor is she now. Only this morning I have heard of a woman, within a four-mile radius of where I sit writing, who soaked her *sari* in oil, and falling upon her dead husband's body set fire to herself; and of another just saved from a like attempt. Who could prevent them? Now and again, as lately in the Punjab or Gaya, cases are brought to light, and convictions point anew to the law; but Police administration Reports do not represent the tale of suttees in any one Province.

The class of woman who for the kingdom of Heaven's sake became suttee before the Act of 1829, still is suttee, either actually in the old-time way, though by stealth and unnerved by the admiration of the onlooker, or in the life of religion and unselfishness. We have all known at least one such Saint living between her house of Gods and the cares of other people, a burden-bearer who bears without railing, nay often with cheerfulness, and who has learnt to live without any hope, save for him with whom she was forbidden to die. Perhaps the living sacrifice began when she was but twelve years of age . . . perhaps she lived to seven times twelve. . . . "What did you do?" I asked of one such, "in the long ago when life pulsed in your veins?" She smiled at me the smile of her who has attained. "There were the children of other people who needed love; there is always my house of Gods. . . . I am a *Swami-bakht* (worshipper of my husband)."

She to whom I refer was loved and honoured, the high priestess, so to speak, of her family. "She was too holy for life's commonplace, so the Destroyer set her free to pray," as said her Father. Yet, she also was accursed, a thing of ill-omen, not to be seen on occasions auspicious, barred then, even from the Temple. If aught went wrong in the house, even her staunchest friend would say: "I must have looked at your face this morning, *Didi*." And, to be the bringer of bad luck, that must be the hard part of the lot of these women. That they keep their faces to the Light, in spite of this, seems to me the very crown of Sainthood.

I have spoken of one type of widow, the rarest; some there are who identify themselves with the thing accursed, who have not the strength, like that other, to falsify the curse by every moment's life of blessed service, many who accept misery as their portion; some who distract themselves from misery by vice or by lapses from virtue. . . . The odd thing is that modern Hinduism, as represented by the Priesthood, would wink at the last-named, while excommunicating the virtuous widow who re-married. I said "the odd thing," but wrongly, for of course, if my earlier conclusion be true, and modern Hinduism is a system of canonical "Thou-shalt-nots" and not of refined ethics (as in the *Shasthras*), the Priests are quite consistent.

"You shall be outcast. I will not dine with you."

It is but another anomaly in this land of anomalies that *that* should be the strongest possible sanction in a community where there is no social intercourse in the Western sense, where individual families live so entirely aloof, that their womenkind do not visit each other.

But the fact is, there is nothing more unassailable than caste. In the second century before Christ Buddha strove to break it down —Gautama Buddha, who was so reverenced by the Hindu that he is considered an incarnation of Krishna. . . . Yet, to-day, in Buddh Gaya, the preacher of the brotherhood of man sits in the beautiful old Temple, to which Hindu and Buddhist alike come on pilgrimage, with a caste mark on his forehead! And under the very shadow of the image the Brahmin will throw away the food or water defiled by contact with the outer-brother.

We see men travelling by the same train (and of course this and all the other cohesive tendencies always being quoted to us do effect something), and we think this represents a breaking down of barriers. Does it, of the real barrier? Listen to the Water-Carriers on the platform: "Water, water for the Mahommedan"; "Water for the Hindu"; "Water for *the Brahmin.*" The Brahmin may "water" any caste, the highest may stoop to serve the lowest; but the highest may not accept service of any but the highest.

To my mind this caste problem is one which will need grapplement before any single other object or aim or ambition can be made national, representative. There is neither speech nor language in orthodoxy, yet its voice is heard by those who live among the masses away from the Anglification of the great cities; and it is a voice that asserts, that none dream of disobeying. It is a voice that curses; men fear to disobey, even when they writhe under the curse. And all the full ecstatic organ stop of the handful of vociferating Reformers in the Metropolis would not drown one silent syllable of its perpetual invocation!

One word more. I have called this study *the Nasal test.* We all know what happens when a Hindu wife lapses from rectitude. There is no scene in a law Court, but she goes through life self-betrayed; she has lost the tip of her nose. The pain of the punishment is obviously its publicity; but it would be interesting to know whether in origin it had any connection with caste. Is it possible that the mutilated nose was but symbolical of the husband's right to excommunicate? "For this sin you are to me outcast. I know no greater punishment. Reap even as you have sown!"

IX

THE MOTHERS OF FIGHTERS

RUGGED hills, all stone and cactus bush, and brown-white dust and grass the colour of dust; and, from the desert beyond the hills, hot dry winds smiting the face. . . . Such is the country which breeds the warrior caste—grim and gaunt and attractive. Nothing of softness in man and soil, even the very fold of the hills where elsewhere in the smiling uplands of the Deccan or the rhododendron-clad Himalayas, or the jungle-veiled hills of Central India, you expect a handful at least of grass, green and succulent for the sheepfolk: even this here breeds stones to hurl at the invader when other missiles fail. The Rajput hill-giant opens his mailed fist and shows you David's weapons.

"Nothing of softness in man or soil." And yet once you are inside those hill-fortresses the grimness relaxes—you get the very romance of beauty—lace work in marble, water palaces and walled gardens. Thus at Oodeypore, at the foot of that wonderful rock-hung fortress of the King who was saved by his Nurse, is the *Suggun Niwas*, sitting like a lotus flower on its broad green leaf—a series of marble lattices and balconies and exquisite turrets, built round the quiet peace of a water garden of fruit trees, gorgeous study in orange and green, or the *potpourri* of the flower garden of my Lady Rosebody. Or there again, is the Queen of Cities, the Universal Mother standing to greet you at the mouth of a great mountain gorge. The road winds higher and higher, the gates of the outer world close upon you; you are at home here in the peace place of "the heart's true ease," beside the lake of pink mimosa and sweet-scented thyme. . . .

You walk in the dead cities—the walls have outlived the rivalry of Kings—the white palaces glitter on the hill tops, and the priceless mosaics still hide in the niches. . . . The fierce upstanding men of the divided beard, their swords girt upon their loins, are fighters still.

You know that when you meet them in the Cities of the Living, they have not lost their cult of the sword, their love for the soil, these earth-born. But, what of the women? The gardens are deserted and the baths and robing-rooms, the summer palaces, and the sandal-wood halls of pleasure, and all the dainty or thoughtful arrangements which prove the Raj-putni an individual in the eye of her lord—all deserted. . . . Here, when the King held his moonlight Durbar on the roof of the palace, she had hidden to watch the pomp and circumstance of feudalism, the glitter of jewelled daggers, the soft richness of brocade, or the sheen of those richer garments of light . . . and the Lake lay peaceful at her feet, and the twin fortresses frowned watch and ward. . . . Here she was suttee when her Lord died fighting at the Gate; here she led his armies to victory; here she drank smiling, the poisoned cup, which was to save the honour of a line of Kings. . . .

Down this dusty road, between the high walled mountains, she walked in the procession of women, all garlanded with roses and jasmine, to make oblation before the Goddess of

Children. Or, now again it is the Festival of Flowers" itself; the grain has sprouted and the women go with singing and dancing to bathe in the sacred Lake before they carry to their lords the green sprig which, worn in the turban, is sign of love and unity. It is the Women's Festival. No man may take part in it; but the grim men of the grim mountains, with love and reverence at their hearts, stand at the salute—a guard of honour for the women as they pass.

Or now she is in trouble—her lord is at the wars, and her little ones are defenceless in the Fortress which overlooks the desert . . . what shall she do? She sends her bracelet, and a strand of silk, a circlet of gold—it is but a symbol, to him whom hereby she calls her Brother, "Bracelet-bound-Brother—and hereafter her soul knows no fear.

And he? the Brother—whose but hers is his devotion, his life; and he gives both willingly, albeit knowing he may never even see the face of her he serves. Not the crassest mind would attach the smallest scandal to the relationship. . . . And perhaps selflessness in love, the love of a man, has seldom in India reached a higher level. . . . And that brings me to a reminiscence.

It was a hot day in an extra oppressive June, and I was making my way through the Bazaar of a Raj Town—to the rabbit warren where burrowed the workers in enamel. The Bazaar itself was full of interest—open-air booths, gay with glass bangles and draperies; quaint ox-carts, tied up in gorgeous red "lampshades" to shelter the bargaining Purdahnashin; wedding processions; priests with begging bowls, and pontifical bulls, small and white and saucy, moving from grain stall to vegetables, exacting toll at will. . . . But my Master-worker had more still to chain me. The artists sat on the roof, dreaming their colour dreams. They told me they worked on the roof because in a busy town you cannot get near enough to the Earth-Mother; and you are reduced to lessening the distance between you and the sky. "What would you?—something living must watch a man at work—if he wants perfection."

They sat before queer little tables; some beat out on the rich gold trinket the pattern which was to hold the colour—mixed to some secret prescription, old as the City, of precious stones ground fine as powder; others painted —their pallet, slabs of brass with five finger marks for hollow; their brush, steel needles. All the light and colour in the sky seemed entrapped in that workshop. And now, suddenly the light has gone, and the workmen grope after their tools and pack them away; and the roof is left to the women and me.

They were telling me a story—the old-time one of that Queen who full of grief at her lord's cowardice in refusing to stand by his overlord, had buried herself alive under a sour plum-tree, which ever after grew and flourished exceedingly in appraisement of her deed. "Tchut"! said one: "Bury herself—what work! Better far have girt his sword upon that not-man, and sent him forth in the name of his Fathers, and of all the fighters yet unborn." . . . And all the other women wagged their heads in appreciation of this sentiment.

Now I had heard that story last in Bengal. But far other was the comment. The Bengal variant tells of the clever subtlety with which the husband avoided the battle, and how it was only the wife's action which betrayed him to the overlord, who said, "Because this woman had shame in her heart for a man's cowardice, the women of this house shall for ever be called 'Queens,' but their husbands shall not be Kings."

And when they get as far as that, the women say: "What! can any desire widowhood? Alas, what little love the Ranee had, not to rejoice that her lord was saved the danger of death! Alas! what defect in love to cast blame upon him in dying!"

But it is never in Bengal that the story is followed by another old as the Sack of Chittore. The Rajput widow is about to spring into the flames when she sees the boy who saw her husband die. She pauses awhile, and "Oh Badal," says she, "tell me ere I go hence to join my lord—tell me how he bore himself against his enemy." And Badal: "He was the reaper of the harvest of battle. I followed his steps as the humble gleaner of his sword, on the bed of honour he spread a carpet of the slain—a barbarian Prince his pillow, he laid him down: and he sleeps ringed about by his foes."

Hearing which she of the warrior caste, goes smiling through the fire to her tryst.

The fact is, you see, the ideals of the women are not the same. Both .have given to the world, do give to the world, new types of perfection in love; but to one, love means the service of the world, and compulsion of the highest in her Beloved to that end; to the other it means just the service of her lord, it means self-abnegation and worship to the exclusion of all criticism.

She of Rajputana although giving royally, demands something, and gets it: she of Bengal demands nothing, she is here to give, not to get; and if by chance she is thrown a crumb, she is grateful to pathos.

The one type, if I may so put it, is masculine, the other the quintessence of femininity . . . and it is a difference easily explained. It is the outcome of the history of the two peoples. The Fighter demands that his womenkind should be of the stature of the Mothers of Fighters. So to the beauty of subjection, she adds the beauty of self-respect. In the other, self is so submerged that there is no room even for respect of self. And, the sainthood of the women apart, one questions the wisdom of the second type, for the man.

The *Khettrya* Rajputni of to-day though very strictly Purdahnashin is still *an individual:* still does she claim and keep the spirit which is hers by inheritance. The festival and practice of the Bracelet has its place in her life even now, though the fighting days are over . . . still is hers the reverence of the Flower Festival. But the custom of the Mahommedan has affected her also: she lives much in the Zenana, attending to her gods, her house, and children.

The *Shudra*, who has no purdah, and the *Veiskya*, whose purdah means two veils and a number of women attendants, may be seen in the street: and, as we look at her in her pretty red draperies, carrying so gracefully her pyramid of water-pots, or trudging sturdily through the burning dust to the shrine beside the Lake —we see in level brow, in frank open countenance and carriage, the spirit of the free —and we say to ourselves, "No! the personality of the Rajputni is not dead, it is only domesticated."

But we carry our questionings no further: "By God, I am a Rajput and a King. I do not talk of the life behind the curtain!"

X

THE QUEEN WHO STOOD ERECT

IT was a spacious roof-terrace—large even for the house of a King: for an earthquake had destroyed almost an entire story, and no one had troubled to do more through the years that followed than move away the *débris.*

So the Zenana had a whole wing of open spaces at the top of the landing, and here it was that we sat, under a sky that was like a pink opal, while the swallows and the yellow-beaked *mainas*, and crows, flew overhead to roost. Bats there were too—"devil's mice" —flapping the sleep out of their wings: and now, a red-brown throated, red-brown coated *brahmini-kite*, to whom the women made prayerful salutation. A kingfisher had just flashed past, bright as the sea at noonday, bright even in that darkening light, and knowing the reverence of the Rajputni for the kingfisher, I thought the gentle courtesy his.

It was *Nanni-Ma*, Baby's Grandmother, she who had the face of victory over death, who explained. "*Kali Ma* chose once to take that form," she said, inclining her head towards the red-brown one. A sudden swoop brought him almost within reach of the baby plaything and those lonely widow-women, and with terror in loving eyes the child was clasped close. Who shall tell what mixture of dread was in their hearts? dread of the big bird's talons and dread of *Kali* the Destroyer, to whom if she wanted a life, that one life which was theirs, it must be yielded, cost what it might. . . . But the love which was the parent and the offspring of that terror was spilling out of their eyes as they handed the child each to each—first Mother clasping him, and then Big-Mother, while the white-sheeted waiting-women huddled on their haunches, cloth drawn beseemingly over mouth, gurgled "Hi! hi!" wagging their heads, and swaying with sympathy. It is unique, the attitude of a Hindu widow to her baby, unique in its beauty even among baby lovers. For the child represents more to these lonely ones than just a soft lovesome bit of flesh and laughter, of pretty pursed lips and rounded limbs, and great mop of soft black hair; more too than the gift of him they love. It is now in itself their passport to heaven, their token of the visit of God to the world: it is to be, presently, the saviour of those who have been closest to them in life—husband, father. . . .

"One small flicker in the lantern of the body—should any put out this light, who will relight it? For us, not even the Creator himself, in this life, not even the Creator. . . ."

And the home of Love was the eyes of those two women as they passed the boy back and forth between them; and the home of tears was their heart.

And he?—darling rogue of but a dozen or so bright fortnights of the moon, would tyrannize in his manhood even as he tyrannized now; nor would he hear reproach in that household of devoted women. Did not his Father likewise?—who, dying, confessed to *Nanni-Ma*, that the sins he had committed would need many sacrifices and much offering of the sacred cake for expiation. And she, blaming him not, set patiently about his bidding, sparing nothing—the one note of joy in that chaunt of sorrow being this: "He came to his Mother, he loved her enough to come, to trust her;" . . . and, as the half-understood regret passed like a shadow over the dying mind, she used all her art to brush it away. "Fear not, my Son; was it not written? Is this not fruit of that past birth of which you have no remembrance. All is illusion even sin; all is good, yes, even sin could we know it . . . and your death-ceremonies shall be to be envied of men, buying you sinlessness through many future births. Fear not. . . . And, when he is of age, the boy, he also shall perform your ceremony . . . a new birth to righteousness. Do not fear, my Son."

It is this memory which is in the soul of Big-Mother, as she plays with her son's son on the terrace in the mystic hour between the lights.

But the boy will grow, and there will be a bride to be found for him. What great excitement this means for the Zenana, few know who have not gone in and out among the women. There is the search among caste folk near at hand, or at a distance. Often the Priest of the family goes a tour to consult the horoscope of likely candidates. . . . There are tragedies when Priest meets Priest and doctors the horoscope to fit desire or sloth; but that chance must be faced by all alike. . . . No need, at any rate, to fear that marriage will take the boy away, it but brings one more daughter to Big-Mother . . . a shy, small person—among the orthodox, aged ten or thereabouts, who keeps eyes on floor demurely the first year of marriage, in the presence of whomsoever; and always, always runs out of the room, or hides face and head, standing reverently in the presence of her lord. Even many years of marriage do not relax this reserve when third persons are by. I have known mothers of grown sons who will carry one aside to whisper what is necessary to be said, but which cannot be said direct to their husbands in the presence of others. . . . "Let the women be silent." That a wife may not take her husband's name is a very general rule throughout India.

Out of all this knot of etiquette, born, it

seems to me, of some distorted view of danger to modesty, as well as of a becoming respect and reverence, it is hard to disentangle the Indian conception of the love of a maid for a man. But this is certain, it is unlike what is the ideal in the West. There is worship; he is her God; he has brought God close to her. She is created to serve him with all her powers of mind and body, to serve and never criticize or question. The habit of her life is expressive of the relationship. The day is planned round his needs. She brings water to wash his feet, cooks for him, anticipates his smallest want while he eats; if he leaves on the green plantain leaf of orthodoxy one mouthful for the faithful slave, how happy she is the day long!

At his hands she holds her life. . . . I remember a poor little woman who had been induced by some modern-minded friend to resent the drunken belabourings of her husband. . . . She ran away to the protection of a relative, and all the Zenana held up hands of horror, not at the beating but at her resentment of it. "What! did she not know that Hindu wives belonged to their husbands, to be done with as they would? Would she not give her body to be burned at his desire? Why not then give it to be beaten at his desire?" And no reasoning would convince them of a difference. That this conception of devotion can rise to great heights one knows. It is not uncommon for a Hindu wife to make way of her own accord for some younger wife, even though retaining her passion of love for her husband, or rather perhaps, if one could conceive it, because she has arrived at Love's perfection. . . . And I have seen her charming to the second lady: "Whom my Lord honours, shall I not love?" But there is little *camaraderie*, except sometimes in old age, when the grandchildren are growing up; there can be little between such differences of levels—and very little community of interest either in work or play—where one is educated and the other not, where one may go about the world unveiled, and the other is hedged round with protection of wall and curtain.

Again, as there is no choice in marriage, since the orthodox marry in childhood, there is little chance for love except after marriage. "We grow up to think that such an one belongs to us," explained an Indian girl to me of her boy husband; "we take the relationship as you do brothers and sisters; you do not choose them; you do not, however, therefore of necessity, resent them." That attitude then is the beginning. That it does lead, as a rule, to loyalty and worship we know; that it often leads to a very high type of love, where each goes with each, all the way, in perfect sympathy, has also been known.

And the man? "English people," said a Hindu to me, "do not understand our relationship to our wives; they treat their wives as we treat—left-handed relations." It is true, the Hindu considers any show of feeling an insult; he almost neglects his wife in the presence of third persons. Necessary courtesies are left to brother, father, trusted old servant. . . . As they grow older she graduates in giving, he in taking. Is he paying the highest price possible to him in—*taking*, I wonder? Who shall say? My own impression is that he does not think about it at all, seeing it has been the habit of generations of Indian men. One does not think about what is natural. The pity is that the standard of ethics is different for men and women—and this surely is wrong in principle. "As you sow, so shall you reap," is orthodoxy for the man. "As you sow, so shall they reap whom you best love—your son, your husband"—is the woman's religion. She reaps herself, yes, but as a secondary result, and her own benefit certainly never enters into the calculation of the individual woman.

Do good if you can, but if you cannot, or will not, stand up to your penalty like a man; or rather lie submissive under the full flood of it. Count the cost, the degradation to the lowest order of creation, the weary re-start through the gradations of re-genesis. At least there has been no deceit. Sometimes you may buy back part of the penalty by counter-balancing good deeds. An Eastern loves a bargain, and the business of salvation is one great mercantile transaction; but only men are allowed on this Rialto.

Vicarious *suffering* with a woman for chief actor is one of the tenets of the male.

Vicarious *pleasuring* with a man for chief actor is the woman's.

I said that you took your penalty, you paid

your price. True, but not always. In the highest scheme of punishment, whether for man or woman, some one else pays. The Gods strike at the thing you love best. If the Gods are angry with a woman they take away her husband. Is not the very treatment of the widow in India recognition of the fact, and does she not so accept it?

But to return to the husband's respect for his wife, that is a good thing to record. Say it is only policy; "where women are honoured, there the Gods are pleased; but where they are not honoured, no sacred rite yields reward." . . . Say it is grounded in the fact of her being his possession; possibly, but at any rate it is there. How pre-eminently he regards her as his *property* there is proof upon proof. He leaves to no other hand punishment for encroachments; he shuts her away, lest eyes of others who do not own her should see and covet—it takes more than one generation to kill the anger in the eye of a man at a glance of admiration from another, honest though it be; and when he dies she remains his property still, that is the reason of perpetual widowhood; and till it was forbidden did she not, as suttee, acknowledge that she was his property, useless when no longer needed?

There is a temple on a City wall in a country of sand and low scrub, gray with dust. The Temple is beautiful with its outlook on the sea of sand, and the little earth holes of water where the women dig in the sand. It is a Temple to a woman. She was beautiful beyond words, and Kings sought her in marriage, and fought for her with the King to whom she was betrothed. And at last one of the Kings slew the Betrothed, and claimed the hand of Ranak Devi. But she, rather than betray the trust of him whom she had never seen, but whose she was nevertheless, sought refuge in suttee. It is her Temple which you find on the City wall, and round about it have gathered other women—there is a very forest of Suttee Stones. You may know them by this sign—the hand and arms of a woman graven in the stone, always the right hand, palm outwards.

And you find here also the *pallias* or memorial stones to warrior Kings and to great rulers among women. For the place of memorial stones, of the dead, of silence, is a place of glory. To it come the bereaved, the empty-handed, to give thanks for those who have attained; to it come the young, bending beneath blessings; death and life walk ever hand in hand, and the white jasmine triangles of the newly-wed make a fragrant carpet in the Temple of Memory.

But one cannot write truly of the conception of Love in any nation without writing a book without end of the conception of each loving soul in its loneliness and aloofness. And, when I said this to my Wisest of the Wise, she made answer: "So it is, even so" . . . and there was such beauty in her face that I wished it had been possible to hear her parable of Love. But silence of words was between us, naturally, on the things we most held sacred.

And it was one who sat by who took up the thought.

"There was a King who loved his Queen with all his soul, and one day, overcome of this love, he fell at her feet in an ecstasy, even in the presence of the of wives, who being jealous, said: 'Shameless he! lift up the hands of the King to your hea '

"And the King said: 'Yea, my Queen, so

even shouldst thou, when I have done thee this honour.'

"But she stood erect, smiling gladly. 'Nay,' said she, 'not so; for both feet and head are my lord's. Can I have aught that is mine?'"

XI

PORTRAITS OF SOME INDIAN WOMEN

TAKE first the Indian wife. Was there ever the world over a like conception of the married state? Chief priestess of her husband, whom to serve is her religion and her delight. One with him in the economy of the household, certainly, but moving in a plane far below him for all other purposes—religious, mental, social; gentle and adoring, but incapable of participation in the larger interests of his life, incapable of participation even in his games.

"We are richer," "we are poorer"—that the bounds of a joint intelligence. To please his mother, whose chief handmaiden she is in things domestic, and to bring him a son—these her two ambitions; but the latter chiefly, for to the mother of a son will a husband forgive even wrangles in the house-place.

Oh, the worshipping of Gods, the consultings of oracles, the stealthy working of charms to this end! And if the Gods prove gracious, proud indeed is the little lady, a creature of good omen, a being to be welcomed at feasts, to be invoked by the childless. No longer is she a failure; even widowhood would leave her with the chastened halo of that son who is worthy to offer sacrifices.

Such an attitude of mind may seem irrational to the alien, but it should be remembered that the whole idea of marriage in the East revolves simply on the conception of Life; a community of interests, companionship—these never enter into the general calculation. Nor is this strange when one reflects on how large a place life must fill in the thoughts of a people believing in re-incarnation. As a life-bringer alone has a woman her place in the scheme of Hindu philosophy. For life and religion are inextricable in the loom of Time; and woman never did have a Vedic value.

Look at her, then, our little Hindu type of wifehood—gentle, submissive, a perfect house-mistress, moving softly about the women's domain, "the Inside." Up with the dawn, she bathes and worships, worships her own special godling and tends her sacred plant, then draws from some ancestral well the water for the household needs, scorning no domestic duty. A picture good to see is she on these occasions—her pretty red draperies girt out of harm's way while she heaves aloft the shortening rope with subtle grace. Mark the poise of head, the turn of slender wrist, as the first shafts of daylight strike brilliance from mystic amulet or jewelled armlet. Further domesticities occupy the day, with perchance a little gossip in the house-place ere the evening meal brings fresh need for a skilful house-mother. She waits upon her husband while he feeds; silent in his presence, with downcast eyes, to look him in the face were bold indeed. Perhaps he talks to her of village or family interests; she would not think it strange did he not.

The boy! Ah, yes, he is a tie. Encouraged by her husband, she will quote his sayings or boast his feats and feignings. But there is no evening home life as in the land across the seas. After feeding, the man seeks his men companions, with their talk or their gambling.

So, watch the little lady clean her pots and hie her safe to bed—content.

I would not have you think the picture one of shadows. Often, and especially where love has entered into the contract, 'tis a twilight study, softly lustrous. A wife respected as competent house-wife, as counsellor, as triumphant mother, sharing her husband's anxieties for the upkeep and shepherding of their little family, aware of his ambitions, if little understanding them, and happy in their joint observance of orthodoxy—that sheet-anchor of safety to her conservative soul. You must be careful how you dress this lady in your picture. Wind her garments about her in established fashion, even to the smallest fold; make the red mark of wifehood on her ample forehead; oil her hair and plaster it tightly down behind her ears; forget not the ornaments for ear, for nose; and never, pray, forget that gold and ivory bangle—"marriage lines" to her. About her toe rings you may suit yourself. Some find them irksome, and anklets jingle pleasingly in any case. You must make her plump, there has been no chance of exercise to tone down outlines;

uxorious, too selfless for vanity; placid, never roused except in defence of her man or her brood, but with a reserve of obstinacy which all the wild horses in the empire would fail to move. She is the true guardian of the past; and uneducated, the true enemy of Progress in India. This is our lady of the middle class. The peasant's wife has compensation, for often she shares her husband's work in the fields, and that makes common topic. Moreover, being unlettered, he has fewer temptations than his wealthier brethren to live an individual life.

For our studies in sad monotone we must go to the wives of one section of the "England-returned," as they are called.

Try to picture this lady. She can speak her own vernacular, perhaps read it, but Western influences have passed her by. Greatly skilled is she in things domestic. She has watched her husband with awe through the throes of his local university, and then he sails away out of her ken to that unknown land beyond the "black waters" of separation. Dimly through the years does she hear of him, and great fears are at her heart as she thinks of the women he must meet in that land of "the unveiled"; but these are fears she may tell to none. What pre-emption can she have in his affections? Then he comes back, wearing a bright pink shirt, an English top-hat, and patent leather shoes. He drives a dog-cart, and divides his time between his office and his club; he dines at English houses—new fears here for breach-of-caste rules. . . . But she worships nevertheless. To buy him blessings is still left to her, and Indian wifehood was ever a school for altruism; but in a family group you will grant the inharmoniousness of the anachronistic.

Let it be ceded here, however, that there is another sketch possible of that "England-returned" one. Some diversity of interests cannot be avoided; but I have known a few little wives whose Anglicized husbands did their best to educate them, led them painfully through the new ideas, brought them somewhat into the "reformed" life.

To myself the attempt has often seemed pathetic, trying "to walk with one foot," to "clap with one hand"; but our little lady is painted this time in a glad luminosity of gratitude that, having seen the world, he should still deign to care.

But sometimes the woman, too, has had chance of Western education. I have known one or two of her kind in Bengal and Madras, more in Bombay. Perhaps she passed through the stage transitional herself once; at any rate, she has arrived all safely, keeping her pretty national dress, keeping also her vernacular. A great part of her day must be re-made for the ceremonies of orthodox Hinduism which she has discarded; yet, something solid she has in its stead, since no influence will ever make a Hindu woman irreligious, thank God.

She will talk to you of the struggles of the great Indian reformers, of Ram Mohan Roy, of Chaitanya. She will separate for you, with true discrimination, the symbol from the spirit in ancient Hindu philosophy. I have even found her reading Jowett's Plato, Emerson, Browning. "My husband recommended these," she explains. Him she companions as sufficiently as does any woman of the West her husband, walks with him, drives with him, and is not watched with hungry, jealous eyes, as are the newly "emancipated" women of other Indian communities, whom some of us have seen abroad for the first time in mixed assemblages of men and women.

Perhaps she is not as good a head domestic as her great-grandmother; but service is merchantable, and, at any rate, she takes an intelligent interest in the education of her children.

This much has Brahmoism (*i.e.*, Hindu Theism) done at its best; and, mistakes apart, it is not a bad "best" for a nation in transition.

The recoil from a too servile imitation of the West is bringing about a wise admixture that may eventually prove really useful to the progress of the nation.

Not yet have I touched upon the strictly veiled woman—the Hindu woman in palaces or of certain parts of India, and the Mahommedan woman.

As queen, she is multiple; subtle tones of colour here, the peculiar living tincture of great joys, great sorrows. I have known her bitter with the consciousness of growing years and barrenness, lording her seniority over her young and beautiful rivals—a shrew for whom surely there is much excuse; and I have known her gentle to her co-wives as to much-loved sisters, admiring of their graces, living with them in kindly, humorous companionship. Nay, I have known better. I have known her at so great a height of saintliness that, her own arms empty, she will pray the gods to grant her rival the gift of motherhood.

Sometimes she is very young. I recall a pretty child of seventeen who came to this particular queendom because her husband was successful in procuring a white peacock!

"You may marry her," had said the King, her father, to the suitor, "if you can bring me a white peacock."

He had not known that such things were, and when the expectant prince produced a spotless ghost-bird, the King, for the sake of his word, had to give him his daughter.

She was very happy in her new home; as it chanced, she was a unit, and not one of a group. She had her own gorgeous apartments and waiting-women. All day she turned over her pretty trinkets and possessions, or made charms against the evil eye, or listened to endless stories from the Court gossip; and at nightfall she played hide-and-seek on the roof overlooking that garden where the peacock had his place of honour.

Sometimes her husband would pay her a visit of ceremony, when she would sit, eyes cast down, to answer his questions in monosyllables. Sometimes she herself would visit her mother-in-law, falling at the great lady's feet in graceful salutation. I have known her very merry when this formality was overpast. These visits were her only interludes in monotony. Yet she was not unhappy. She had expected nothing else, and more light and air fell to her lot than to that of many.

Seclusion is sometimes so rigid that it has been little better than intermural imprisonment from one year's end to another; no garden to stroll in, no chance of ventilation of any kind or sort; no outside interests or companionship. Nor would the women themselves thank you for suggesting innovation. "Did our great-grandmothers live otherwise?" they would ask.

The question now is, how far should the enlightened members of the community strive to better the Purdahnashin custom? In the days when it came to stay in India there were alleviations. You have but to look at the architecture of the older towns, of Agra, of Jaipur, to prove the fact. Every courtyard had its marble lattices, from behind which the ladies of the house, securely screened, might watch the bear and tiger-baiting, the wrestling, the ancient games. They had their private gardens and their baths.

The long pilgrimages in palanquins made change and movement in their lives. The system was less injurious to health than it is now. In a town like Jaipur the whole city is one running commentary in rubric on such alleviations. For the secluded lady there were perpetual peep-holes on to the life of the street, with its daily pageantry and frequent carnivals. The more modern householder builds blind walls in his jealous passion of keeping.

Is it any wonder that the race grows degenerate?

Thrown back upon herself, robbed of air for mind and body, marvel is the Purdahnashin is as nice as we know her.

Take for instance one trait, the loyalty of

wives to their husbands. All who know the orthodox Hindu Zenana will have pathetic instances in mind of a loyalty which dignifies all womanhood. Nor often however, I hope, is loyalty put to such severe test as with the little lady whom I found imprisoned in a fortress in Northern India.

Her story was interesting—she was the daughter of a King, and educated beyond ordinary. "She shall be as a son to me," had said her Father, and he taught her to read and write and figure, and rumour said that even the local magazine was edited from behind the Purdah. When she was of an age to marry, her family Priest went a horoscopical tour to secure her a husband.

At Benares he met the family Priest of another Raj in search of a bride, and the two Priests agreed to end their wanderings, and accommodate each other. But alas! the bridegroom's priest had not revealed that his patron was half-witted, nor that the Ministers of the estate were in negotiation for a lady from among themselves. So, on her wedding day the Raj candidate learnt both that she was wedded to an idiot, and that she had a co-wife.

She afterwards said that the first six months of her life were almost happy, though she did not realize this till the contrast of the afterwards had come upon her. They killed her babies—as they were born, they were both boys—one they smothered in tobacco fumes, the second had less merciful handling. For the birth of the third she requested protection, taking care to explain that her husband was not at fault, "God had made him a fool." She was given a fortress not far from the Capital, a Guard was put on the gate. . . . All this happened nine years before help reached her. In the meantime the Guard had become her gaoler. Food she had none, save the remnants of stores laid in nine years previous; servants or companions she had none. For nine years had she had speech of no one.

Her father had died; all attempts made by her old Mother to get to her, or to get news of her, had failed. Then, in penitence for making the marriage, her old family Priest brought me to her. I have never forgotten what I found at the end of that difficult journey . . . a fortress in ruins, the home of bats, and so unsavoury that the only clean spot was a small roof-terrace furnished with a string bed and a broken chair or two. Here lived the Ranee and her son; he was alive and safe —in this she had her reward; but provisions were reduced to one earthen pot of grain, and endurance was much strained.

She told me her story, with pitiful entreaties not to hold her husband to blame; how could the poor creature, God-blasted, be responsible? The ministers were responsible, who held her liable for the fact that her co-wife had daughters only, always daughters! Even calling the last—"*No more of this* Kalidevi"—had brought no improvement. Yes, she had seen her husband; once he made his way into the Fortress through a private gate while out hunting, and he climbed up to the roof-terrace and sat on the broken bed, and said: "Let me go, lest I be moved to compassion and help you." And she had helped him to go secretly, swiftly, even as he had come.

Poor man, what further proof were needed that he could never be to blame. "Had not God Himself made him a fool? she blamed him not," but I noticed that she devoted herself passionately to providing against like misfortune for the son. We took her servants and supplies, and later brought her away in safety to her Mother. The Fool lives. The co-wife must now be dead, for when last I heard of my Ranee two significant things were reported of her: one was that she worshipped an empty earthen pot with the left hand (that was to show contempt), and then, to protect herself, offered the first mouthful of every meal to an amulet which hung round her neck. And are not both these things known to the initiated as referring to ghosts of co-wives alone?

Yet another type is the woman who rules a State, whether in her own right (as with the Begum of Bhopal), or as widowed regent.

History tells us of one such lady, whose diary of statecraft an emperor of India was glad to consult. Shrewd, wise, far-seeing, responsible, the Purdah has hardly been any drawback to the women born with a talent for ruling, though even for these exists the chief danger of seclusion, namely, that they may get to view life through the eyes of one person —their chief adviser.

Where he is unreliable and the woman is weak the danger will be apparent to all.

It is the chief adviser who rules in reality, manipulating her revenues, surrounding her with creatures bound to him by ties of relationship or purchase; as likely as not her spiritual guide is also of his choosing, and the lady is in a coil from which extrication is well-nigh impossible. I have seen her struggle to get free, and fall back again helpless; but most often she is dangerously unconscious of the subtle influences abroad. Her day is spent grossly, lying on her elbow among brocaded cushions, chewing betel-nut, while her maidens fan her, or amuse her with tales of Court rivalries and jealousies. Her Prime Minister brings her documents to sign, and she hears perhaps an occasional account of his administration of the estate, but there is no sense of obligation towards her people; no interest, even parochial, in their daily life; no thought for their welfare. It is not to the advantage of the chief adviser to encourage feelings of this kind, and the woman herself has too little imagination to care about the wants of subjects whom she never sees.

But all Indian widows do not rule estates. What then of the rest? What of the ordinary widows, of the highest caste, for instance, the type of woman who, in the olden days, would have fed the flames of the funeral-pyre bound to a husband's corpse? What of her.

For the most part she lives the life of a willing drudge in the house of her mother-in-law. "For it is so alone now," as one explained to me, "that we can win merit for our lords."

I have never forgotten the agony of this little lady, sent home to her own mother to live in luxury, robbed of her chance of service.

It is not, I think, untrue to say that the orthodox Hindu widow suffers her lot with the fierce enjoyment of martyrdom and a very fanaticism of selflessness. But nothing can minimize the evils of that lot. After all, a widow is a thing of ill-omen, to be cursed even by those who love her. That she accepts the fact makes it no less of a hardship. For some sin committed in a previous birth the Gods have deprived her of a husband. What is left to her now but to work out his "salvation," by her prayers and penances to win him a better life-place in his next genesis? So even the "cursings" of her are in their way a satisfaction. They are helping her to pay her debt to Fate.

For the mother-in-law what also is left but the obligation to curse, exaction of that debt? But for this luckless one her son might still be in the land of the living.

Now, how shall I make it clear that there is no determined animosity in this attitude? The person cursing is as much an instrument of Fate as the person cursed. Are we not all straws blown by the wind of Fate, and of our own past actions? Little room is there in Hindu ethics for the sense of personal responsibility for wrong-doing.

Indeed, the widow is often, especially as she gets on in years, and in the house of her own mother, a person loved in spite of her fatal gifts of ill-luck. She fills the place of a good home-daughter, is at the service of everyone, from the eldest to the youngest. Often she is a devotee, most religious, and greatly supported by the consolations of her faith. She will herself say on some occasion of rejoicing: "Let me not be seen, I am luckless."

And there is certainly no denying that the sum of self-sacrifice which she represents is, at its best, some solid good to a nation—the salt leavening the lump. One can imagine how the practice of suttee helped to maintain this high Hindu ideal of altruism, so comparatively easy was it to face that one final act of pain and of glory. But in these days, and under the petty tyranny of a mother-in-law, the altruism of the little widow is worn threadbare.

It is all very well in theory to assert no personal animosity towards her whom you hold it a religious privilege to curse, and to burden with every unpleasant duty imaginable. Your practice is apt to mislead. Even Hindu widows are but human, and a lifetime of such dissembling of love must leave them slightly bruised at the foot of the stairs.

Again, with the laxity of modern times and the lapses from orthodoxy, there comes to the chief sufferer the wonder whether after all she is dealing vicariously in this spiritual rhialto; whether she is buying gifts for her husband after all. The morbid consciousness that she is a thing of ill-omen gnaws at her. Admit the doubt and you admit inability to bear what is put upon her; you admit discontent, consciousness of hardship, of ill-treatment. Yet all these tyrannies, this very doubt, has the march of time brought to the Hindu widow. There lies the tragedy. From whatever cause, she is losing faith in her own sacrifice, in her old attitude towards life; and therefore is she to be pitied indeed.

How can we help the fact that the number of women in this class must increase daily? The age marches forward towards personal and individual dignity, and the old ideals of the vicarious are being pushed into the background of the unregenerate.

The majority suffer in silence; some gloriously, some ingloriously and sadly rebellious. Some fall into the hands of the Widow Remarriage Committee, and are re-married. It is not for the onlooker to say whether this solution is sufficient. A few are now beginning to find that life has some use for a woman unmarried, even for her. They are learning to earn their own living and to bless the world with honest labour. She is buying back the curse, this widow who works, in a way which must surely conserve for the nation much of that selflessness which we claimed in the suttee, and certainly much more apparent usefulness. As doctor, teacher, nurse, and in humbler walks of life, which of us who know modern India have known and not blessed the Hindu widow? For the first time, too, since the Vedic era, do we find in India unmarried girls over ten years of age. This is the nearest approach to spinsterhood in the East, and the spinster—she is very rare—is almost always a self-respecting woman earning her own living.

I have said that the impetus of the age is towards individualism. How can we keep the Hindu woman out of the great current?

The time when the nation could be served by a grovelling womankind—if ever such time there was—is past.

A woman's place in the National life will now best be filled by the realization of herself; she must grow to her full stature, taking as her due her share of God's light and air, of the gifts of the Earth-Mother.

She need lose none of those qualities which made her loved in mythology, in the times of the Vedas, in history. Indian women have it within their power to prove to the world that gentle womanly graces are not incompatible with independence.

What a redemption of that curse of the widowed, what a revenge on Time, if the widow herself take the foremost place in this regeneration of Indian womanhood!

XII

GARDEN FANCIES

EVERYONE in India is familiar with the homely little *Tulsi*—the sacred basil—with its aromatic brown spirals and dull green leaves. It was sprawling across the drive of a house I had newly come to tenant, and while my *Mali* and I did tidyings in the Garden, I spoke to him gently about the plant. "Move the sacred garden-person. Suppose some day we drove over it and hurt it, quite by accident, what sin! See, put it in a new hole yonder, by your own hut if you wish." He is a holy man, my *Mali*, from Puri, where dwells Jagannath of the Car with his Brother and Sister; and he will not touch the *Tulsi* till he has bathed, saving for it his first draught of water of mornings. I could only hope that my good intentions were credited. But he made no sign beyond a reverence to the *Tulsi*, and a wagging of his head from side to side, which I interpreted as "Forgive me" (to the plant), "do I not eat the Huzoor's salt? It is an order" (for me).

Notwithstanding, the *Tulsi* moved not, and frequent reminders at last elicited a reason. "It would take a ceremony and a very holy man to transplant the sacred *Tulsi.*"

"Bring him; make the ceremonies," I entreated, stipulating only that I should be present.

So, next morning he brought the holy man, and they sat, both of them on their heels, beside the bush, and read it some sacred texts about Jagannath and his colleagues; then they explained to it the situation, my wishes, its own danger . . . and with many mutterings of magic words they carried the plant to the new place.

The rest of the ceremony was fixed for "the hour of union," and when all was ready I was duly summoned. Little earthen pots, fed with oil, in which floated a cotton wick, made great illuminations about the Mali's hut.

The *Tulsi* sat in its hole, and gathered about

it in apology and propitiation were the Mali's gardening tools; the basket, mouth to earth, holding a light, a brass plate of sugar biscuits and parched rice, and a pot of Ganges water. . . . He made an offering of the tools and foodstuffs, and last of all of a handful of lovely white lilies. These he crushed among the brown roots, bruising them, burying them—who shall say what symbol he had in his mind? then he watered the plant, muttering, and finally settled once more on his heels and read it a little pink book of invocations to the God of the Car—read it from cover to cover—there by the light of the little earthen lamp on the basket.

When he made himself into a huddled-up pillow before the tree, head pressed against the newly-raked earth, I knew the ceremony was over. What was most extraordinary was his utter unselfconsciousness. He had been pleased that I should come, had begged it; but at his "God-worship," my presence was completely forgotten. The ritual was more than form of game. How cruel to suggest to such as he, then, the thought in my mind, that the *Tulsi* probably owed its sacred origin and place in every Hindu courtyard to its efficacy in keeping away mosquitos!

I wondered what reason my Purdahnashin would give me for the worship of the *Tulsi*. I would ask. Curiosity was rewarded with a beautiful story. Why did she hold the *Tulsi* holy? It was only because it was the wife of the Great God. Did I not know the tale? Listen then. Once upon a time lived a great Giant who had a beautiful wife, and was successful in conquering and possessing himself of everything he wished.

In his pride of conquest he forgot all limits and claimed the wife of the Destroyer himself. Then the Great God, angry, came himself to earth to punish the Giant, and slew that powerful one as he lay beside his bride in all his security of possession. But when the poor lady walked forth to make living sacrifice of herself, as was meet, upon the dead body of her lord—it was the Great God himself who was enamoured of her, and he sat by the burning corpse disconsolate. None could drag him back to heaven; nor moved he night and day till the object of his love had found new form in the sweet-smelling *Tulsi*, with its soft green leaves and brown flowering spirals, struggling upwards to the light.

"Forget not the perfume of the *Tulsi*. The customs of your race, in marrying, in dying, in loving . . ." sang my friend. "It means all that to us who sprinkle it with water in the morning."

* * * * *

But in my little garden there was no holy *Tulsi* to sprinkle with water in the morning! Transplanting suiteth not the aged: and the friend of the Garden-people appeared before me sad and shaven.

"My Mother is dead, and at my hands: have I leave to carry her to the waters of oblivion?"

Leave, of course: but let the blame be rightly fixed; not the worshipper, but the Huzoor, she who ordered, carried the sin. This did not satisfy, as I would have wished: and it was not till many days later that the faithful slave brought me a cleared brow, and his mountain top of philosophy.

"But to him who does not deem it sin it is not sin."

Now is that what the sacred plant will now say henceforth and for ever to my lover of ceremonies in his garden, and am I responsible for the dangerous doctrine? I wonder.

XIII

A CHILD OR TWO

IN an orthodox Hindu house of mine acquaintance are to be found two darling Babies, aged four and five. They are girls, one named "Lightning-Beloved," the other after a Greek Goddess.

I made their acquaintance first in the Summer, and they were most seasonably dressed in gold waist-bands and an amulet a-piece—for the Goddess of Learning, a bear's claw, and for "Lightning-Beloved," a little gold box of mystic "spare-me-s" against the blue sword of her tempestuous Lord. . . . I was much in request for games, and daily beguiled into longer and longer visits; how could one resist Babies who were just being introduced to the joys of childhood? And, when I left the "Inside," there would be one Baby on my hip—they taught me that, and it is quite easy,

I assure you—and one clinging to leg and hand as I walked downstairs.

But joy was at the full when I invited them to come and see me. The hour fixed was at a distance of a week, and every day I was asked "has it come?" When it did come I was sitting at my window, and seeing the Raj carriage and pair, with all its pomp of liveried attendants, dash up the drive, I smiled to myself, thinking of the semi-nude atoms which would presently issue thence. Little did I know. The atoms, my very own Baby friends of the waist-band and necklet, were translated. At the door, hand in hand and very shy, stood two of the quaintest oddities I have ever seen —*my* Babies, sure enough, but dressed as English widows, crêpe veil and all, with long false curls of rusty black hair adown their poor little black-gowned backs. Oh! but how I laughed! And they stood by, rueful and disappointed, while I stripped them, even to their natural clothing.

"Then the Miss Sahib loved not the English clothes; nor" (with a gasp of wonder) "the hair of another."

"*No! No!*"

And two pairs of brows knit themselves in solemn puzzlement over this contrariety. Then, "But the Miss Sahib said she loved the children people of the English."

"Yes! what then?" (but I had guessed). "We want the Miss Sahib to love us." . . . The darlings! Then it was all made clear, helped out by the *Amla*. They had, even as they said, laid their little plot to win love. They would dress like the children-people of the English. But how to compass this! Their Mother undertook to arrange; and a clever *Amla* went to a second-hand clothes shop near by, which often supplied Theatrical Companies. "No! they had no dress of the English children-people; but stay—an English Mem-Sahib had sold them a dress not long since. They could make two small copies of this." And the Babies were reproduced in the sad image of some English widow (curls and all), who had evidently fallen on evil days or the brighter days of second marriage, and got rid of her panoply of mourning.

I think my Goddess of Learning and "Lightning-Beloved" know by now that these foreign arts are unnecessary in the way of love. I have had no widow repeats, but in my heart I hide the realization of a pathos and charm hitherto unsuspected in the consciousness of Babydom.

It was in connection with "Lightning-Beloved," whose Mother was seeking a husband for her four-year-old, that I came across the "orphanless child," as he was described in a petition. She explained to me that as she was sonless, "Lightning-Beloved" must be married quickly to someone without fortune or family, though of the right caste. He would then be even as her son, and be supported by her in return for the honour of an alliance. This extraordinary position, "domesticated son-in-law," as it is called, has been accepted even by adults, and is very familiar in Bengal. I know of one instance where a man waited to propose to the lady of his choice (it was a reformed Hindu family), till he could prove himself capable of supporting her, only to discover that a younger and rather lazy brother had forestalled him by accepting the position of the "domesticated." However, it was useless arguing the indignity of dependence with "Lightning-Beloved's" mother, and one's only chance lay in expounding Sanskrit scripture as to the possibility of waiting for marriage till a later age. Unfortunately, it is a question of Priest-gifts desired at this particular moment, and counter-texts are produced for my consideration, proving that delay means risk of a first-class heaven; so that nothing but the woman's faith in my assurance that I will use my influence with the spiritual Powers to secure her the coveted position, nevertheless, saves the situation.

For the Goddess of Learning is desired an adopted son, heir to a Raj. I am pleased with this choice, the boy has a face like Rossetti's Blessed Damozel, and a charming disposition; and we have just been in time to save a threatened repudiation of him by his adoptive Mother. It would have been a dreadful thing, for having by adoption lost for ever all spiritual rights in his natural family, he would, on repudiation of adoption, be left without ancestors for whom to pray; and this, for a Hindu, is terrible indeed.

A new little settler has lately sought the shelter of this Raj, a six-year-old Baby in self-protective exile from her own Estate. Under local law she succeeds as the only unmarried "female" to a considerable inheritance, and as a consequence all around her, grandmothers and sisters included, are interested in her death. They have been drugging her, and she has been brought into headquarters under Police guard. I found her in a wretched house set down in a swamp, and furnished with a hard plank-bed and a box. "Lotus-born," that is her name, is a miserable shrimp of a Baby, arms like sticks, and a plaintive long-suffering little face, like a cry for help sounding in my ears to this day. She was very ill indeed, burning with malarial fever, and aching, she said, in every limb. She lay on the hard "*takht-posh*," and beside her sat her nurse, another baby, eight years old. She sat like a frog, legs crunched up, and her nursing consisted in giving the sufferer a loving pinch every now and then, murmuring, "There! that makes it better." And the six-year-old, in a monotonous little voice which struggled after cheeriness, would answer, "Yes! Oh! yes."

I found that the Nurse had tied herself to "Lotus-born" in friendship by a ceremony peculiar to this part of the country. Two tanks are dug, contiguous, and the children make a play with fishes and boats, floating them in the water, and offering rice and feastings on the grass. Quaint songs are sung.

"Who is worshipping the water with garlands of flowers while the sun is overhead?"

"It is I, chaste and virtuous, lucky sister of a Brother. May I have sons who will not die."

But "Lotus-born" lived not long enough to find fulfilment of her prayer. Better nursing came too late, and the petals of the Lotus curled together in eternal sleep.

* * * * *

The mother of "Lightning-Beloved" is in great spirits this morning. The son-in-law elect was ill, and I had pointed the moral about letting children get past baby troubles before you betroth them; it is so one lessens the risk of widowhood.

"Well! at any rate," she said, "you should be pleased with me. Your 'Lightning-Beloved' is not yet a widow. I saved her from being *born* a widow."

This was startling, but I waited explanation.

"When 'Lightning-Beloved' was on the

way to life," she said, "there came a Guru from a far country who told my Guru of a game the women play there. Two women who are friends, and are about at the same time to be dowered with the life-gift, betroth two balls of flowers. If both children are of the same sex there is no result of the ceremony, but if of opposite sexes and one die the other is a widow. . . . She may even be *born* a widow."

"But you would not hold to that?"

"Where it is the custom who can escape? Yet 'Lightning-Beloved' was not born a widow; for this I should have praise from the Miss Sahib."

"But it is not your custom."

"What matter? I should have praise. She is not a widow!"

* * * * *

I was musing sadly on children-widows that morning, because of a story told to me by a friend. Someone visiting a local prison was attracted by the misery of a woman who had murdered her child. He spoke to her, and she said she wished that her own life had been taken, for she loved her child, and all she had done was to right the wrong of early widowhood. "Her husband died when she was five. Do not I, who have lived a lifetime of widowhood, know what that means? Was I wrong to try to save her from misery like to mine?"

In truth, apart from the written law, it is difficult to judge the woman. She loved her child, and in her own opinion did no more than pull her gently away from under the wheels of that Jagannath Car of Hindu widowhood.

There was my "Dog-girl," now just dead, poor child. What of her Mother? she who has made war upon her only daughter since her second year. What of her? There is no law to meet her case. What of her? "God has not said a word."

It is a graphic quarrel in three generations of women, and of women living in the same Palace, only a courtyard dividing each from each. Sullenly they lived, silently year in year out, not a single interest coming from the outside world to distract their attention from their hates and resentments. Traffic indeed with the world they had none. Palace walls shut them in securely, shut them in with their broodings and bemoanings, with the intrigues and loyalties of their several waiting-women, and with one gray-white *Sarus*, the red-throated, a ghost-bird, walking restlessly on his high stilts from courtyard to courtyard.

I saw the solitary creature first in the cow-dust hour before the stars come out, and he seemed to me somehow the embodiment of that quarrel, the lost soul of the inharmonious.

I have said the quarrel was in three generations—daughter, mother, grandmother—and, of course, like all Raj quarrels, it had been made by a third person to suit his own purposes. My connection with it was an attempt at Peacemaking, when the daughter was about fifteen, and could speak for herself. Not soon shall I forget my journeys . . . flat, mud-coloured country, with mud huts rising out of the ground, as if you had pinched up the earth into hiding holes . . . mud-coloured humans like detached pieces of their own houses herding undersized goats, or urging miserable beasts and an unwilling plough over the baked earth: little vegetation, but here and there a palm-tree, standing straight and solitary against the heat-hazed, pewter-coloured sky, as if even Nature had need here to throw herself on God . . . This was before the rain. In a week all was changed, the road was under water, and I had a weird, mysterious drive through the rivers of streets. The suspicion of a moon was overhead, and a glorious fresh breeze wandered the world. Silently we drove, *swish*, *swish*, fifteen miles of—a call to secrecy, as if all the world had finger on lip—"*hush, hush*" . . . . the trees said it, the feathery bamboos whispering head against head, and the soft gray clouds, and that veiled moon, and that wistful breeze, and those muddy streets, they all said "*Hush!*" . . . even the bare legs of the saises, as they ran by the carriage, seemed to say the same. "*Hush!*" . . . All the world was slipping into a delicious forgetfulness and oblivion, and there was none to see, none save I, thrilling with sympathy, and that palm or two against the horizon looking on stiff-necked and aloof as if refusing to have part or lot in this flirtation of Earth and Cloudland. I did not mind the palms. I hugged myself with the delicious feeling of being in the secret of the world-things. Once or twice in our pathless journey we passed through a village, so close that I could reach a hand and scratch a soft pink nose of cow or buffalo at its tethering. The peasant householder lay stretched in his winding-sheet asleep on the unguarded threshold. No reason for worry or watch-dog when all your wealth is in dear Mother-Earth, guarded by the floating fluid come down from Heaven for that same purpose. How good will be the rice crop after this soaking he knows full well, that slow-minded one who sleeps so blissfully.

But it is after midnight, and we have arrived. And next morning there are secrets again, but of a different kind, in the air, and my work is cut out for me.

It was the little daughter who was most difficult to manage. "How could she visit her Mother? she would be bewitched. Had they not on such-and-such a day—it was the fifth day of the dark fortnight in the month of the Spring games—had they not, her Mother's minions, thrown mustard in her path as she walked? Did the Miss Sahib not know that *that* was a powerful breeder of demons?

Oh! but yes! Colman's mustard that you get in yellow tins from Europe shops. . . . And,—"once they bade her to a 'peace-making meal,' but there was poison in the food . . . How did she know it? Oh! she was not without sense, who does not know poison when they see it!"

The Grandmother spoke a more forcible tongue; charges under the Penal Code, with quaint excursions into the family history of the past for parallel to this unworthy widow of her son.

The Ranee herself was dignified. You can afford dignity when you hold the purse-strings, and your accusations take the form of reduced allowances. She entertained me much this lady. As soon as word was brought her of my arrival she went to bed, feigning sickness. How did she know what manner of woman I might be! It were best to be on the safe side; if you were ill and in bed you could, with courtesy, avoid seeing visitors. So she went to bed. But she sent her Prime Minister and her most confidential officers to call upon me, that they might report. Was their report favourable, or did curiosity get the better of discretion? I know not; but early next morning a long procession of Palace servants in red and gold liveries came with gifts of welcome. Each man bore a tray of fruits and things auspicious; one touches the trays, leaving a silver coin behind. They bore also a letter of compliments praying an early visit. "Such was the beneficent nature of my visit to her State, she was well. . . ." For me, after writing back elaborate congratulations on the quick recovery, I stood at the window watching the messengers. Their lithe, smooth bodies glistened in the sun, and on each tray reposed the red and gold livery of that visit of ceremony! Once through my gateway, what need to carry superfluous mark of civilization.

The days that followed brought their own burden . . . visits, morning and evening, to this lady or that at the Palace, and visitors calling all day, each one with some tale against his neighbour, some story of Court intrigue. . . . "Where all is unknown, best be on the safe side and accuse" was their motto. And silent patience in the hearer led to this much knowledge at least, that there was one man's name held in detestation by all alike. . . . And when the sun set there was solitude, and I walked in the Temple Garden, a garden which was a wild bed of Indian jasmine and other sweet-scented flowers loved of the gods, or played with the children of the old Priest at the Monkey Temple; or anon, sat still, in the cleft of some low branch, while the Priest himself told legends of the country-side—quaint tales of miraculous cures, or gruesome tales of living corpses. . . . And once an old Mutiny soldier recited Persian verses to me in a voice that should have reached his old battlefield at Delhi, many miles away; and once again, on a dark night of stars, they showed me the King's games of by-gone days—little green parrots turning somersaults in circles of fire, and torch-bearers dancing a wild tattoo. . . . So the days passed. . . . Of what account was Time to the believers in Eternity? They would not be hurried. But every day we gained ground, and at last all was ready for the great peace.

Etiquette of the strictest was imperative: it needed some care to secure this without friction. As a personal favour the old Grandmother promised to come with me to the

Ranee's apartments; likewise the little daughter clinging tightly to my hand for fear of those same mustard demons.

As a personal favour also, the Ranee agreed to welcome her Mother-in-law in orthodox fashion.

Five o'clock of an afternoon, and a long dark room lined with waiting-women standing erect and silent, each waving a huge glittering fan planted like a flag in front of her . . . *flap*, *flap*, went the fans, like an elephant's ears; and the serving-women's ornaments shone like stars on arm or forehead. I had just arrived, the first and third generations in either hand, myself a little fearful as to possible backsliding. The old lady I seated; then going across to the Ranee at the other end of the room, "Your Mother-in-law," I said, "has come to visit you. May I take you to her?"

It was thus, you see, we adjusted reconciliation, met each other half way, without too much sacrifice of pride . . . and, as I led my Ranee forward, "I want to see," I whispered, "if your 'falling at the feet' is as pretty as ours in the West Country." "Prettier," she said. "Look!" And, covering her face, she fell three times at the feet of the old dame, who stood there stern as an irrevocable sin. And she? She might have blessed the prostrate woman, but, at least, she cursed not; and so as not to strain forgiveness too far, I made excuse of heat and else, and had her conveyed back to her own courtyard.

The Mother and daughter were less ceremonious; the Mother wept much, and to seal the peace, made over to her daughter jewels of gold and precious stones, silver palanquins, silver bedsteads, silver toilet sets . . . all of quaint Indian patternings—the jewels, magnificent sets of emeralds and pearls, of rubies and topazes—nose-rings, ear-rings, armlets, bracelets, circlets for hair and forehead, decorations for the little bare feet, showers of emeralds and pearls falling from a band round the ankle, over the instep, and ending in a ring for each separate toe.

And behind the Curtain sat the Prime Minister and Treasurer reading a list of the gifts —a *price* list! totalling item by item, calling "Is it there?" "Is it there?"

The darkness deepened, we finished our

inventory by the light of tall brass lamps—cotton wicks floating in open pans of oil—the handmaidens still lined the walls, still waved their jewelled fans. Once the daughter spoke. "A pearl is missing in this nose-ring!" she said. . . . Do not be hard on her, my poor little dog-girl. At first, I will own, I was so myself, chiding her gently for her attitude. All she said was, "I have known my Mother since I was two years old." Then wonderingly, "So the Miss Sahib thought her tears true tears!"

* * * * *

Later I saw more of the child, and watched her grow human and childlike. The "dog-girl," I called her, because she had a passion for dogs, would rescue the most mangy pariahs off the streets and care for them herself, fearless of consequences. I promised that my own dear "Chow" should visit her, but as he was, I explained, a high-caste dog, it could only be when the outcasts were out of the way! It was so I got rid of the yapping pack in the days of heat; but watching from her window, one later day of hail and thunder-showers, she saw some ill-treatment in the street, and re-admitted the "outsiders from Caste." It was on this occasion she rebuked me. "Is the spark of life in Caste-Brother and outcast, in Chow dog and Pariah? Then why should I not care for these?"

"But you are a Hindu, Caste is your religion?"

"That is man's invention; where man has not invented, let me hear the voice of God calling me to have compassion on a fellow life."

And now she has heard the voice of God calling her out of this life of fellowship, perhaps, who knows, in supreme compassion of her own little stunted, shadowed life of high-castehood. . . .

So, after all, God has spoken.

* * * * *

I had taken these thoughts out for a walk on a sunny day in the hill country, and had now arrived at my destination, where I meant to leave a card.

It was a house which boasted an electric bell, and unlike Indian houses, had a closed door, overlooking the street. As I pressed the button two hill children, in blue and red kimonos, and long plaits of hair, stood watching me.

"Poor Miss Sahib," said one to the other, "she is pressing a piece of wood, and thinks to open the door that way."

The babies came nearer. "Poor Presence —pressing the wood at the side," and they laughed.

I turned round and smiled at them, which gave the younger courage. "Doors," she said, "open not with pressings of wood at the side; by the turning of yellow balls in the middle do the foreign people open doors. We have seen with our eyes."

Then, as if apologizing for instructing me:

"Shut doors were ever a foolishness," she added, and ran away.

XIV

THE TIE THAT BINDS

"THE Hour of Union"—with the west, a red gold lake of fire, turning to the colour of smoke—there, behind the tall gray steeple from which comes the Christian's call to prayer.

The crows which have been so noisy all day long spread their wings for flight; the palms across the road and the great star-flower tree at my gate are among their bedding places, I know of old. All things travel toward the Silence, and my soul stretches herself at ease, up here in the open spaces of my roof.

What is it saying, the Christian Bell? "*Vivos Voco: mortuos plango: fulgura frango,*" speaking its unknown tongue to a people that understandeth not, nor wishes to understand. *Vivos voco, vivos voco.* . . . But no bell calls the Hindu to worship. She worships when she will, not necessarily in groups; she rarely passes a temple without worship, most often just silent prostration: sometimes she will creep in and ring the bell that hangs beside the bull, her timid call of ceremony on the god: or she will run in to leave a flower, or to comfort her heart, poor soul, with prayer for the moment's need. Nor need she pray always in a Temple. I have seen her light a light at cross-roads—the very tragedy of a prayer—among the wheels of traffic in a busy town, a special prayer this, for a new little life that is to be. *Vivos voco*. . . . No need to call where religion is not imposed, rules of a school whose head master is God. The head master will punish infringement of those rules, so teach the ushers sometimes. . . . But to the Hindu sin is not an offence against any Being; it is but putting one's self out of harmony with one's highest attainment. Do it, an you will, you anger none. You but travel so many more rounds of the wheel of life . . . on and on . . . on and on . . . reaping in the next cycle what you have sown in this . . . Oh! the weariness of the pain of birth and re-birth! Oh! the helplessness of trying to escape.

There *is* no escape. Life is inexorable. Life is more inexorable than Death.

*   *   *   *   *

And now the gray overhead is tinged with rosy pink. How long after the sunset lives the memory of the sunset? This is the marriage of day and night, the twilight hour, the time of affection, the time of peace. . . . Now the clouds are staining the great roof of the world —their bridal congratulations. Soon, they also will have fallen back upon silence (for is not colour speech after its kind?) and then the God of Night will sprinkle stars all over the floor of the bridal chamber where day and night lie hiding while we sleep. For while we sleep, night walks with day in three great strides across that star-strewn floor, back to the east where we find her again. "As the Sun sets, but never dies, even so shall the Sun of my Life set; but I shall not die." . . . "*Mortuos plango*". . . . But why wail if I do not die? Death is release: death is but the next chance: the new start. Who wails the dead? going where all the sunsets go to come again, even as they.

Say I have done evil: well! I made my

choice. Now I go to pay like a man. Say I have done well: I go to my reward, through the same door as had I sinned, for but two doors has this House of Life for all, the same exit the same entrance. And but two doors will have the next house, and the next . . . the many mansions on the way of Peace. For Peace comes *at long last;* there is always that; we may make it come now, this minute, if we choose, if we lay aside desire . . . "He attaineth Peace into whom all desires flow as rivers flow into the Ocean, which is filled with water, but remaineth unmoved . . . not he who desireth desire."

But, the chances are endless, why come so soon to the Peace-place. Let us enjoy all enjoyment, this house and that, *and that* . . . Oh! the weary wander to the House of Peace. Oh! the loneliness of the way: for none may hold my hand as I walk. None may even be my sponsor. No man shall save his Brother's soul. This journey to God, to Peace, must be my own journey of discovery. Oh! the loneliness of this constant converse with Fate! It is the loneliness which men are wont to associate with death: when the Eastern ceases for this—dialogue—he has attained Heaven, absorption into the Divine. . . . Oh! the loneliness! Oh! the joy of loneliness and solitude; the joy of aloofness, each for each. The Soul and God together, alone together side by side, and at last, alone and one . . . one Great Soul. For our souls are carrier pigeons, homing to God. *Mortuos plango.* No, the carrier pigeon has brought its message through all the worlds, to God Himself. The pigeon rests at peace in the home of Light.

Fulgura frango . . . Fulgura frango. But what need to break the lightning, what need? What is, is good; what happens is ordained. Fight not with Fate. Love it. Conquer by loving it . . . Never resent, never resent. Submit to the evil, and behold it is good. All is illusion in a world of dreams; who can tell if the lightning be good or bad? Better not break it, lest worse befall; better not.

* * * * *

Even as one looks the illusions of vision are fading, steeple, trees, house-tops, are only blurs of grayness, and the other voice of prayer smites the stillness—"There is no God, but God" . . .

Beware, beware of resisting Fate; beware, there is who kills and who makes alive. None may oppose Him; why break the Lightning?

* * * * *

Oh! the time Between the Twilights is good: one floats on the sea of silence, and is nothing—just part of the Great Creation—absolutely at rest, at one with Nature, at peace with one's self, with one's neighbour.

Shall we remember in the next House, the furnishings of this? I asked of my Wisest of the Wise.

"It will be as you desire, as you intend," was the answer; and then, musingly, "Most wish to forget, most wish to forget." . . .

There is in her the strangest mixture of ritual and freedom from ritual. That is because she is a woman. Hinduism, as we find it in India now, is but a tradition, of which the women keep the record. You may believe what you will, there are no articles of belief, there are idols for the ignorant, there is poetry, allegory, which you may interpret as you will; there are the beautiful songs of the *Bhagavad Gita*, there is the propitiation of evil spirits, there are the extortions of the ash-smeared;

there is the ecstasy of the wife-worship of Life, of her husband, her child. There is the crown of self-sacrifice, and there is the demand of the stronger for the service of the weaker. All stand for Hinduism; but none connote Hinduism. Of its essence is caste . . . and here we are back again at our marriage register. The one fear of the Hindu is, lest so-and-so will not marry into his family. If he does that which would prevent marriage he has ceased to be a Hindu. . . .

And the things which might prove a bar to marriage among Westerns do not of necessity prove here a bar to marriage. There is no excommunication for sin; there is excommunication, out-casting for breach of a ceremonial rule. The man under Western influence may be ashamed of a son-in-law who has served his time for a crime. Not so the orthodox Hindu: has he not paid the penalty for his sin, why cast it up against him? That account is closed.

If you wish to know what things would outcaste, ask the women. They have learned from their grandmothers, and they from theirs.

In the long ago travelling Priests would

wander from house to house, telling tales from the old Epics, or building up that great fabric of folk-lore which we find in all parts of India. Often they would act the tales they told or sing them, and this made great entertainment in the lives of the women—Mystery Play, Oratorio, brought to their doors. In these latter days your Priest will whisper in your ear the name of the God you must worship, and he will direct your worship, and chiefly your charity; but he gives you no bundle of ethical maxims, no credo: and in a woman's private chapel her own temperament supplies the religion. As I have said, most usual is the worship of the Baby *Krishna*, though there is also the Shiva cult which I have described, both with the same idea running through them, the reverence for Creation. Then to the timid, religion is often but a faggot of superstitions—what to avoid, what brings luck . . . every home provides some old dame learned in this lore.

In one thing, however, all are alike. They will keep faith with Gods, not always with men; that matters little, for no one has taught them that sense of honour, product of the self-corporate, got from living in masses in the world. But the Gods are another matter, the Gods can punish. And the courage with which the frailest will keep faith, at what cost, offering a child in performance of some vow to a Temple, measuring her length along the ground in pilgrimage . . . this is one of our paradoxes in India.

In the lives of most there is room for little beside the worship of the husband, with its perfection of self-sacrifice, which seems to exhaust all of altruism that the religion holds. And that is perhaps the chief difference between the standpoint of the West and Hinduism. When you benefit your fellow-men, it is more to buy merit than out of compassion. I suppose compassion dries up at the fount, so to speak, in the consciousness or sub-consciousness that misery is only another illusion, that in a way you have elected the present suffering, that at any rate you might have the very best of times in your next genesis. But however it may be, philanthropy among the orthodox is an acknowledged soul-saving arrangement. Listen to the very beggar in the street. "Gift me and buy merit," is his prayer. He is not ashamed to beg; you are climbing to heaven on his shoulders. In a way it is you who are in his debt.

This absence of altruism is a fact which experience is always emphasizing; and I deem it the more noteworthy, inasmuch as in the field of thought and meditation the heights climbed are very great indeed, it is quite common to come across a mysticism parallel to the mysticism of the West. But I would not be misunderstood; though the doctrine of works and merit is the most general kind of Hinduism, I have met a higher. "Good works are fetters of gold, but still fetters," as said my orthodox interpreter of religion, and he went on to explain that even the desire for goodness could be an obstacle on the way to God. Whereafter he told me this beautiful story.

There was once a woman who had lived an evil life. She was a Mahommedan, and she said to herself, "I will go the Pilgrimage and wipe out my sins." So she set forth, taking with her a dog she loved. And as she wandered, her face Mecca-wards, the other pilgrims shunned her, for they knew her ill-repute. But she heeded them not, her mind being full of the so-soon purchase of sanctity. . . . And it came to pass that a few miles from Mecca the dog fell ill, and she said within herself, "I cannot leave it behind. I must needs stay and tend it." So, albeit with a sigh, for Mecca was almost in sight, and she had longed so great a while to be holy even as those other women by whom she was shunned, she turned away from the path in search of water. But it was a place of sand, and it was long before she found a well, and then she had perforce to make a rope of her hair and a bucket of her clothes to draw water for the poor beast . . . and, in tending him, day changed into night, but she heeded not—her whole soul in the desire that he might live.

And when the pilgrims reached the Holy City, and were preparing for the evening prayer, a voice forbade the recital . . . . "This," said the Voice, "is not the place where God is to be found; go back to where she whom you deem evil tends a fellow life, for there to-day dwells God Himself."

Faith is naturally a large factor in the religion of the Hindu women. Belief is so easy to her. She is troubled with never an intellectual doubt. Indeed, intellect, in her opinion, is an interloper in the regions of Faith. Where is the scope for Faith if you use your intelligence? she will argue.

There is a story told, one of many such, of a South-Indian woman, who believed that upon a certain day of the new moon, the God at a certain shrine would work whatever miracle were claimed by the faithful as a proof of his power; so, being drunk with ecstasy after long years of meditation, she set forth to the Shrine, having first cut out her tongue. . . . "My tongue which has often," said she, "spoken words of unwisdom, will be given me anew of the God. This is the miracle I claim." Day after day of her pilgrimage she trudged cheerfully, joy in her God at her heart. Day after day she carried but her water gourd and a small quantity of grain tied in the end of her saree, and she walked with the help of a tall bamboo pole, for she was bent with age; but the wisdom light streamed from the gates of her body, so that all knew her for holy, and crowds gathered about her, curious as to the faith that was in her, but she heeded them not; day after day through tracks of burning sand, through jungle or by river bed . . . and at last the temple was in sight.

* * * * *

The miracle was that her faith failed not when her tongue did not grow. After the first shock of realization, her mind groped after some explanation which satisfied, and the God lost no worshipper.

So, in Western India, I have known one—a Queen and a daughter of a King—also bowed with years, who had waited half her life for the fulfilment of a promise.

God would see to it that the promise was kept. Why waste resentment on him who seemed a breaker of promises; God would resent for her. She was brought to the verge of death, she had long been the house-mate of poverty; her faith was proof against all. When I saw her last she sat among the squirrels on a dung-smeared veranda in a courtyard, where cows and buffaloes were stalled. The squirrels played about her; she had been herself a squirrel, she told me, in her last generation, wherefore they loved her; and she sat telling her beads as she had sat for fifty years, her hand in the embroidered sock of orthodoxy.

Had any devil prompted me to suggest to her justification for unfaith, I should simply not have been believed. For—of these is the kingdom of heaven.

* * * * *

One more memory stands out from the crowd. It is the lamp-lighting hour in the Temple of the Foot. We have come through the narrow streets, past the sellers of old brass and copper, past the gold and white pyramids of flower-sellers. The air is heavy with the perfume of jasmine, the sacred bulls are sauntering up the steps from the river, pushing through the worshippers with the arrogance of the beloved. A kind priest has lighted us under the archway, and we are in the inner courtyard. Yes, we may come through the forest of columns, standing straight and white and cool in the cloisters, and we may linger close by the great carved door to watch the *pooja.* It takes some time to see in the darkness . . . everything is still, so still. There is a great basin of black marble, and in the middle of it the impress of a great foot. . . . A priest sits on his heels beside the basin, anointing the foot with sandal-wood oil, washing it, offering it flowers and incense.

Another Priest walks round and round the basin crooning *mantras*. The real worshipper is a poor woman in an advanced stage of leprosy, the flickering light from the little shells of cocoanut falls upon the masses of white and yellow flowers, upon the fruits and incense, upon the costly offerings, upon the poor mis-shapen face. It is still, so still, so full of mystery, her face, the flowers, the Priest, leaping into life like a pulse-beat, with the flare of the cotton wick. . . . Shiva's great white bull sits watching his master's symbol in the Temple beside us: other worshippers there are none, and the *pandas* have wandered to the bathing ghat, to encompass the unwary. . . . Sudden my soul hears through the stillness the message of a child in the strains of that beautiful anthem of Stainer's. His voice rises clear and exultant so that I can hear it across the seas from the Cathedral of old gray stone in the City of Cities. . . . "God so loved the World." . . .

The Priest is passing the shell-lamp over the foot itself, in the circles of some ritual, and the leper bends forward out of the darkness to see the sacred markings. . . . Oh! the horror of the ravages of the flesh! . . . "God so loved the world." . . .

The Priest sprinkles the foot with holy water, spooning it out of his copper vessel with practised hand, and the perambulating Priest redoubles his *mantras*. . . . The face of the leper is a-quiver with peace, and with a joy that is without dissimulation. . . . "God so loved the world." . . .

The *pooja* is over, the officiating Priest has pressed the little cotton wicks into darkness. The leper makes her timid way out of the Temple, ringing the great bell in the cloisters, as she returns to her pilgrimage of pain in a world of illusions. . . . "God so loved the world," . . . and it was the leper in the Temple of the Foot who first gave me a glint of the probable meaning of these glad tidings.